Japan's Practice of International Law

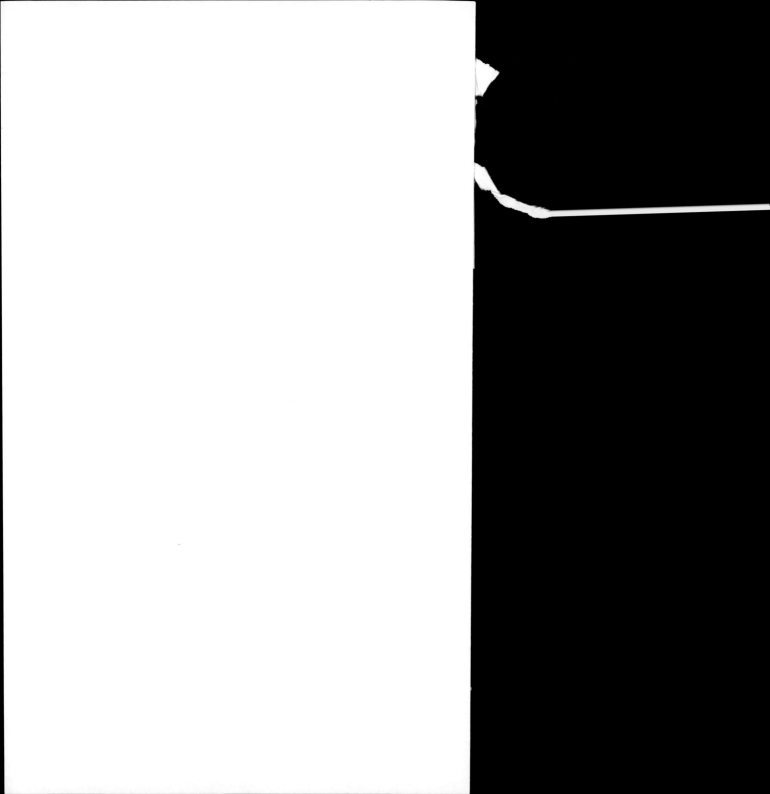

JAPAN'S PRACTICE OF INTERNATIONAL LAW

Hidehisa "Harry" Horinouchi

Ambassador of Japan
to the Kingdom of the Netherlands

LEIDEN UNIVERSITY PRESS

Cover design: Andre Klijsen
Lay out: Friedemann BV

ISBN 978 90 8728 396 4
e-ISBN 978 94 0060 441 4
DOI 10.24415/9789087283964
NUR 828

Printed and bound by CPI Group (UK) Ltd, Croydon, CR0 4YY

Voor Sabien

Contents

Foreword

It is a great honour to write the foreword to Ambassador Horinouchi's book, which makes important contributions to international law.

I have known Ambassador Horinouchi for more than twenty years. When we first met, he was the Director of International Agreements in the Treaties Bureau of the Japanese Ministry of Foreign Affairs, and I was a professor of international law at the University of Tokyo. He took the excellent initiative to organise a group of Japanese scholars to study WTO cases, and I agreed to be its chair. The group had several successful meetings discussing and analysing international legal issues raised in WTO cases.

Ambassador Horinouchi graduated from the Faculty of Law of the University of Tokyo and entered the Ministry of Foreign Affairs in 1980. In the Ministry, he has held a number of key posts dealing with international legal affairs, including the Director of International Agreements, the Director of International Legal Affairs, and the Deputy Legal Advisor. He is thus a well-known specialist in international law in the Japanese Ministry of Foreign Affairs. In addition to the posts indicated above, he has served, among others, as the Minister Extraordinary and Plenipotentiary to China, the Consul General in Los Angeles, the Ambassador Extraordinary and Plenipotentiary to Cambodia, and the Ambassador Extraordinary and Plenipotentiary to the Netherlands. He is fluent in English and Chinese. Besides his regular duties for the Ministry, he has been very active in teaching international law to young people. He has held teaching positions at Waseda University, among others.

As a specialist in international law in the Japanese Ministry of Foreign Affairs, Ambassador Horinouchi has dealt with a number of international legal issues concerning Japan. This book is a collection of articles on selected international legal issues. Written in his personal capacity, the book does not necessarily represent his government's view. The book addresses various issues, including self-defence, post-war legal issues, chemical weapons, the law of the sea, consular immunities, and hijacking. Ambassador Horinouchi analyses these issues from a practical point of view. He is a prominent practitioner, as well as a scholar, of international law. As a coherent whole, this book ably represents "Japan's Practice of International Law" and remarkably portrays international law in action from a Japanese practitioner's perspective.

Judge Yuji IWASAWA

International Court of Justice
The Hague, July 2022

Chapter I

Security and the Right of Self-Defense

8 Hours on September 11

Introduction

The terrorist attacks in the United States on September 11, 2001 clearly showed the existence of a "new threat" to the entire world and that the traditional idea of "deterrence" did not apply. The fact that a private group of terrorists managed to attack the political, economic, and defense centers of the United States at about the same time using multiple hijacked commercial airliners gave an opportunity to completely change the post-Cold War US strategy.

Approximately three hours after the incident, US President George W. Bush said at Barksdale Air Force Base in Louisiana that "the United States will hunt down and punish those responsible for these cowardly acts," and announced the United States' intention to take decisive action against the responsible terrorists.[1] Eight hours after President Bush's remarks, the Government of Japan held a Cabinet Security Council on September 12, at 9:30 a.m. Japan time. After that meeting, Prime Minister Koizumi held a press conference in the prime minister's office and said, "We, Japan, strongly support the United States and are determined to spare no effort in the necessary assistance and cooperation."[2]

How did Japan understand the US intention in light of international law? That understanding has led to the decision of strongly supporting the United States at the initial stage, and later became the basis of the Act on Special Measures against Terrorism. In this paper, I would like to try to verify how the Japanese government tackled the proposition of exercising the right of self-defense against large-scale terrorist acts by non-state actors and how we organized the issues under international law.[3]

As the director of the Legal Affairs Division of the Treaty Bureau at the Ministry of Foreign Affairs of Japan at the time of the 9/11 terrorist attacks, the author was directly involved in the evaluation of this situation under international law and the drafting of the bill for special measures against terrorism. However, the views expressed in this paper do not represent the views of the Government of Japan, except for the direct citations such as the official announcements or answers to the written questions at the Diet.

First appearance of the paper: "8 hours on September 11" in *Law that transcends melting boundaries (2). Security and international crime*, University of Tokyo Press, September 2005.

I. Occurrence of situation and start of examination

1. Initial action of the Government of Japan

At 8:46 a.m. on September 11, 2001, American Airlines Flight 11 crashed into the north tower of the World Trade Center in Manhattan, New York, and 15 minutes later, United Airlines Flight 175 crashed into the south tower of the Trade Center. The towers started to be wrapped in flames. At 9:38, American Airlines Flight 77 flew into the Department of Defense on the outskirts of Washington. Furthermore, at 10:10, United Airlines Flight 93 crashed in the suburbs of Pittsburgh. The north and south towers of the World Trade Center collapsed around 10:30 a.m. US President George W. Bush appeared in front of reporters in Sarasota, Florida, at 9:30 a.m. shortly after the airplanes crashed in New York, and said "Two airplanes have crashed into the World Trade Center in an apparent terrorist attack on our country."[4] (All are US Eastern Time.)

Immediately after this large-scale terrorist attack, the Ministry of Foreign Affairs of Japan set up a countermeasure headquarters in the ministry at 10:30 p.m. on the 11th (Japan Time) to collect local information, grasp the situation, and respond to the inquiries from outside including the confirmation about the safety of Japanese people through the night. Then, in parallel with this series of activities to protect nationals, the Government of Japan began a study on the expected response of the United States and the possible position of Japan.

2. Expected response of US

The terrorists attacked the World Trade Center and the Pentagon, which symbolize the prosperity and might of the United States, at the same time and the number of casualties was reported to exceed 5,000. In this situation, it was very clear what kind of actions the United States would take next. In other words, to a greater or lesser extent, it was inevitable that the US would take a response centered on military action eventually. The problem was when the United States begins military action, where would it place its legitimacy under the international law?

On what grounds does the United States justify the use of force under the Charter of the United Nations, which generally prohibits the use of force? Various predictions were possible theoretically, such as whether to seek discussions at the UN Security Council or to adopt a Security Council resolution that allows the use of force. During examination at that time, the Government of Japan made near-convincing predictions about the basis of the international law that the United States would rely on. Namely, in such a situation, the United States would never seek a UN Security Council resolution on the use of force, but would use force as an exercise of its own right of self-defense. So why did the Japanese Government have this kind of "confidence"? To clarify this point, we must go back to the August 1998 bombing of Sudan and Afghanistan by the United States.

3. 1998 bombing of Sudan and Afghanistan

In the summer of 1998, Washington was in a storm of domestic politics. The focus of the American people's interest at that time was just on whether or not the issue of the relationship between President Clinton and former White House Intern Monica Lewinsky, which had been discovered in late January of the same year, would develop into the second impeachment of the president in United States history.

Had there been a sexual relationship between the president and the former intern? Was the president "lying" to the people? Did the president's testimony under oath in the Jones case constitute perjury? Did the president incite the former intern to perjure? The president's fight with the independent prosecutor Star continued. On August 17, President Clinton testified at a federal grand jury and finally admitted that he had an "inappropriate relationship" with the former intern. In a television discourse that night, the president expressed regret for having "misled the people".[5] Three days later, on August 20, the federal grand jury invited former intern Lewinsky to determine whether the president's act of trying to keep the relationship secret was perjury or contempt of court.[6] However, this news did not make the front page of *The Washington Post* the next day.

On the 20th, US military cruise missiles bombed a terrorist training camp in Afghanistan and a chemical plant in Sudan. The attack was allegedly in retaliation for the terrorist bombing of the U.S. Embassy in Tanzania and Kenya on the seventh of the same month, and was explained as a blow to the terrorists' network led by Usama Bin Laden, a Saudi-born Islamic terrorist behind both terrorist attacks.[7] As always when the U.S. military takes action, both Republican and Democratic parliamentary leaders swiftly expressed support for the president's decision. U.S. citizens' support for air strikes at both terrorist facilities reached 70%, and as a result, President Clinton survived the immediate crisis of the sex scandal hearing. Then, in addition to the strange timing of the use of force, the United States made her own assertion about the basis of international law.

4. Invoking the right of self-defense against terrorism

The U.S. Government explained that the attack by the cruise missiles, which President Clinton called "retaliation" ("strike back"), was an "exercise of legitimate self-defense."

On the 21st, one day after the bombing, the U.S. Department of State held a briefing session for the diplomatic corps on issues under international law, and I participated from the Embassy of Japan. I had thought that the justification for the bombing by the U.S. military would come from "reprisal by force", so the State Department official's explanation was even more shocking. "The United States has acted pursuant to the right of self-defense confirmed by Article 51 of the Charter of the United Nations." "We have convincing evidence that further such attacks were in preparation from these same terrorist facilities. The United States, therefore, had no choice but to use armed force to prevent these attacks from continuing." "These attacks were carried out only after repeated efforts to convince the Government of Sudan and the Taliban regime to shut these terrorist activities down and to cease their cooperation with the Bin Laden organization".[8]

In a situation where the reality of the terrorist network led by Usama Bin Laden was not yet clear to the Government of Japan, there was no way for us to determine the existence of "convincing evidence that further terrorist attacks were in preparation". However, the message from the United States was crystal clear that the cruise missile attacks were not "reprisal by force" responding to the terrorist bombing of the U.S. Embassy in Tanzania and Kenya, but the "exercise of the right of self-defense" to prevent the imminent infringement approaching the American people.

On the other hand, there was no full explanation whether the exercise of "self-defense" against acts of terrorism is permitted under today's international law, whether the requirements of the UN Charter were met, or even if it was a legitimate exercise of self-defense for the United States, whether there existed an obligation for Sudan and Afghanistan to accept air strikes. In the end, the Government of

Japan only expressed "understanding" regarding the use of force by the United States.[9]

5. Challenges for September 11, 2001

The challenges faced by the Government of Japan on the night of September 11, 2001, when the terrorist attacks on the United States occurred, were clear from the above circumstances. The question was whether the Japanese government could legally support the claim of "exercising the right of self-defense," which the United States would (probably) rely on in initiating military operations. With the images of the collapse of the World Trade Center in New York being repeatedly shown on TV, would Japan be limited to the vague statement of "understanding" again? Tokyo, the earliest morning city in the world, had to answer this question first. Naturally, it is not permissible to wait for the attitudes of European countries. Regarding issues under international law that could not be answered in 1998, such as (1) whether it is permitted or not to exercise the right of self-defense against a private group called a terrorist network, (2) consistency with the UN Charter, and (3) the relationship with the sovereignty of the country where the terrorist organization is located, the Government of Japan had just eight hours to reach a conclusion.

II. Summary of issues and conclusion

1. Whether permitted or not to exercise the right of self-defense

Regarding the *right* of self-defense, the Government of Japan has traditionally taken the position that a country has the right to use the minimum and necessary force under customary international law, in the case where there is no other appropriate means to eliminate the infringement of imminent injustice against the state or the people.[10] These are the so-called "three requirements for exercising the right of self-defense" in Japan.

However, as a question before concretely examining these three requirements, is it permissible to exercise the right of self-defense, which is a concept under international law that mainly governs the relationship between sovereign states, against entities other than states? It will be necessary to answer this question from the theorists who raised this point.[11] This point was not a big problem in the examination within the government at that time. One reason for this was that even the conventional interpretation of the government did not take the position that the entity that commits "imminent infringement" must be a sovereign state. In addition, the international community had accumulated examples of exercising the right of self-defense under the UN Charter, for protection of nationals in foreign lands. If one's own people are left behind in a foreign country where security has largely deteriorated due to the occurrence of riots, it is widely seen that military aircrafts are dispatched to rescue one's own people under the circumstances where the consent of the country concerned cannot be obtained.[12] In this case, it is not realistic to change the legal structure by distinguishing whether the subject of the infringement of imminent injustice against one's own people is a state or a group other than a state, and no country is actually making such a distinction either.[13]

Therefore, when examining the legitimacy of the actions that the United States would take, the question was not whether or not the entity that carried out the terrorist attacks had been a "state", but whether or not the three requirements for exercising the right of self-defense existed.

(1) Presence of "infringement of imminent injustice"

At this stage, that is, at midnight on September 11, 2001 (Japan Time), the background of the terrorist attacks was unknown, and as mentioned above, the Government of Japan was trying to confirm the safety of Japanese people, collect local information, and grasp the situation. However, Usama Bin Laden's involvement had been suspected from the beginning. He had been allegedly involved in the 1993 World Trade Center Building bombing incident, had announced a "declaration of war against Americans" in 1996, and had been wanted by the FBI in connection with the 1998 bombing of the US Embassy in Tanzania.[14] If this terrorist attack had been carried out by a terrorist organization centered on Usama Bin Laden with such ability and organizational power, the reality that the same organization was running terrorist camps and conducting daily training to carry out terrorist attacks targeting the United States and American people was considered sufficient to constitute an "infringement of imminent injustice".

Even in the conventional interpretation of international law by the Government of Japan, "in a series of terrorist attacks", "in the situation where the same thing continues happening one after another", where "such a situation has not ended yet" or "during such a situation itself", it has been acknowledged that exercising the right of self-defense may be justified.[15] The real horror that the terrorist attacks on September 11 showed to the world was enough to justify such exercise of self-defense as "infringement of imminent injustice".

(2) Whether or not "there is no other appropriate means to eliminate (infringement)".

Even if the infringement of imminent injustice actually exists, the requirement for exercising the right of self-defense is not satisfied under the circumstances where the infringement can be eliminated by appropriate means other than the use of force. Other such means include diplomatic efforts by the parties concerned, persuasion by the countries concerned, criticism of the international community as a whole, etc., but the most powerful of these measures is the binding decision of the UN Security Council. There is no objection on this point. In fact, since the 1998 bombing of the U.S. Embassy in Tanzania and Kenya, the international community repeatedly worked on the Taliban regime, which had been tolerating the existence of these terrorist organizations centered on Usama Bin Laden. It was in the 1998 UN Security Council Resolution 1214 (1998) that the entire international community for the first time clearly made such an accusation. In this resolution, which focused on peace in Afghanistan, the Security Council expressed that it had been deeply disturbed by the continuing use of Afghan territory, especially areas controlled by the Taliban, for the sheltering and training of terrorists and the planning of terrorist acts. The Council also demanded that the Taliban stop providing sanctuary and training for international terrorists and their organizations.[16] In the following year, the Security Council issued Resolution 1267 (1999), determining that the Taliban's failure to respond to the demands of Resolution 1214 constitutes a threat to international peace and security, demanded that the Taliban turn over Usama Bin Laden without further delay and decided on economic sanctions until the Taliban fully complied with the obligation under these resolutions.[17] Furthermore, in 2000, the Security Council adopted resolution 1333 (2000), deciding to strengthen sanctions on the Taliban.[18] Resolutions 1267 and 1333 were adopted as binding decisions under Chapter VII of the Charter of the United Nations, but the Taliban authorities neglected both of them.

It is recognized that such circumstances are sufficient to judge that the "appropriate means other than the use of force" to eliminate the "infringement of imminent injustice" had already been exhausted.

(3) "Exercise of the minimum and necessary force"

The use of force that is permitted when there is "imminent infringement" and "there is no other appropriate means to eliminate it" must be the "minimum and necessary force" to eliminate such infringement. This is, for the Government of Japan, the third requirement for exercising the right of self-defense. It was, of course, impossible at midnight on September 11, 2001, to see what action the United States would actually take when it embarked on the use of force. However, the United States is Japan's only ally and the two countries reaffirmed their faith in the purposes and principles of the Charter of the United Nations in their bilateral treaty. Therefore, it was not expected that the United States would exercise its forces beyond "the minimum and necessary" level without regard to the restrictions of international law.[19]

2. Relationship with Article 51 of the Charter of the United Nations

Based on the above examination, it was recognized that the United States was allowed to exercise its right of self-defense in response to the terrorist attacks. However, if the Government of Japan expressed its support to United States' military action, an examination based upon the customary international law only would not be enough and we needed to sort out the relationship with the provisions of the Charter of the United Nations. The issue raised here was the relationship between the terrorist attacks and Article 51 of the Charter of the United Nations.

Article 51 of the UN Charter states, "if an armed attack occurs against a Member state of the United Nations," and the Government of Japan had taken the position that this "armed attack" meant "a systematic and planned use of force against one country".[20] The occurrence of accidental or single-shot terrorism cannot be understood as an "armed attack" provided for in Article 51. Therefore, the focus was on whether or not these terrorist attacks on September 11 could be interpreted as "the systematic and planned use of force against a country".

Through the examination, we concluded that these terrorist attacks were fundamentally different from the cases of terrorism in the past. Because these attacks included (a) attacks on the US mainland, (b) attacks on US government agencies such as the Department of Defense, and (c) had a high degree of organization and planning such as attacking multiple targets of the United States by hijacked aircrafts at the same time. Therefore, these attacks were recognized to correspond to the "armed attack" referred to in Article 51 of the United Nations Charter.

3. Relationship with Afghanistan's Sovereignty

When the possible military action of the United States met the requirements for exercising the right of self-defense under customary international law and was recognized as being compatible with the Charter of the United Nations, the final issue considered was the relationship with the sovereignty of Afghanistan. Even if it became clear that these terrorist attacks were carried out by a terrorist organization centered on Usama Bin Laden, is there any issue with the sovereignty of Afghanistan if the United States uses force against that country? Or is Afghanistan obliged to accept such armed attacks?

The overall situation of international terrorism was very different from that at the time of the bombing of Sudan and Afghanistan in 1998. The series of UN Security Council resolutions since 1998 (Resolutions 1214, 1267, 1333) have led to widespread recognition of the Taliban's responsibility. However, these series of UN resolutions stipulated economic sanctions for the international community as a whole, and did not allow the use of force. In addition, ignoring the series of binding UN Security Council resolutions does not justify the use of force against that country. Therefore, in considering the relationship with Afghanistan's sovereignty, a separate examination under international law was required.

The conclusion on this last issue was drawn by returning to the essence of the right to self-defense in the Caroline case. In the Caroline case, which formulated the requirements for exercising the right of self-defense, US Secretary of State Daniel Webster showed the condition with which the territorial nation (US) might accept the use of force against activities unrelated to the intentions of the territorial nation (assistance of Canadian rebels) as justified. As in the case of the Webster Letter,[21] whether or not it is recognized as a legitimate exercise of the right of self-defense should be judged in light of the three requirements for exercising the right of self-defense. As far as these requirements were met, it was judged that there would be no problem under international law regardless of the intention of the territorial nation.

III. On the morning of September 12th

The conclusion obtained through such examination is that "if the United States takes military action in response to the recent terrorist attacks, it is possible for Japan to support it under international law." Reaching this conclusion, however, was only the beginning of verification. In Europe and the United States morning would come after Prime Minister Koizumi's statement of clear "support for the United States" to the outside world. The examination on the eve might have been completely off the mark, and this might not be a case of invoking the right of self-defense, but a case of seeking consultation at the Security Council. Or the act by terrorist groups might not be regarded as an "armed attack" in Article 51 of the UN Charter at all. The day of September 12 began, with the anxiety that the governments of Western countries and the UN Security Council would make different judgments on those issues.

1. North Atlantic Council Statement

On the same day (September 12), the North Atlantic Treaty Organization (NATO) held the North Atlantic Council in Brussels. The Council discussed the terrorist attacks on the eve, and agreed that if it is determined that this attack was directed from abroad against the United States, it shall be regarded as an action covered by Article 5 of the Washington Treaty, which provides for the exercise of the right of collective self-defense. The statement issued after the Council meeting, referring to Article 5 of the Washington Treaty, clearly stated that this attack falls under the category of "armed attack" against one or more Allies in Europe or North America, which shall be considered as an attack against them all.[22]

This decision was the first time that NATO had agreed to exercise the right of collective self-defense since its establishment in 1949. It also had epoch-making significance in international law that Western countries are in agreement that a terrorist attack by private groups can be recognized as an "armed attack" under international law, which meets the requirements for invoking the right of self-defense.

2. UN Security Council Resolution 1368 (2001)

It was the response of the UN Security Council that was awaited after Western countries made the same judgment as Japan on issues under international law. Russia, China and other countries might make a different judgment from that of NATO Members. If the Security Council issued any statement without mentioning the exercise of the right of self-defense, and if the Security Council took a position of continuing to consider the use of force in the future, it would show the existence of a serious division on the evaluation under international law over the terrorist attack that shook the world.

However, such concerns proved to be unfounded. UN Security Council Resolution 1368 (2001) issued on September 12 referred to Article 51 of the Charter of the United Nations in its preamble. By revisiting the "inherent right of individual or collective self-defense" in accordance with the Charter, it showed the Security Council's recognition that this terrorist attack falls under the "armed attack" and the requirements for invoking the right of self-defense are satisfied.[23]

It was the moment when Japan, the Western countries, and the international community as a whole showed their unanimous evaluation and judgment under international law regarding this hateful act of terrorism.[24]

3. Enactment of the Act on Special Measures against Terrorism

On September 19, the government announced "Japan's measures for responding to the terrorist attacks in the United States" and started drafting an act for special measures against terrorism.[25] The act would show consistently the above-mentioned understanding of international law.[26]

Specifically, the title of the act and the description in Article 1 of "attacks by terrorists that occurred in the United States on September 11, 2001" reflected the understanding that this terrorist attack falls under the "armed attack" in Article 51 of the Charter of the United Nations. In addition, the reference to the series of UN Security Council resolutions revealed how "appropriate means other than the use of force" had already been exhausted.

Furthermore, regarding the U.S. armed forces that would take operational action in connection with this terrorist attack, we described it as "the United States and other foreign troops that contribute to the achievement of the purpose of the Charter of the United

Nations by removing the threat posed by the terrorist attack." In the background of this, there was a judgment under international law that these troops were exercising their right of self-defense in order to eliminate "infringement of imminent injustice".[27]

The Parliament of Japan reaffirmed the evaluation and judgement under international law as well and the Act on Special Measures against Terrorism passed both Houses after about 60 hours of deliberation on October 29, 2001.

Epilogue

On October 7, 2001, two days after the Government of Japan submitted the Act on Special Measures against Terrorism to the Diet, the United States and the United Kingdom launched attacks on al-Qaeda bases in Afghanistan. In accordance with the provisions of Article 51 of the Charter of the United Nations, "Measures taken by Members in the exercise of this right of self-defense shall be immediately reported to the Security Council," the United States and the United Kingdom reported to the UN Security Council on the same day.[28] The President of the Security Council issued a press statement on October 8 and revealed that members of the Security Council had expressed appreciation to the presentation made by the United States and the United Kingdom.[29]

From midnight on September 11, the conclusions reached by the parties concerned in the Government of Japan in the extremely limited time available turned out to be in agreement with the judgment of the entire international community, and this evaluation under international law became the basis for Japan's participation in international cooperative action. The world situation following the Cold War is changing rapidly, and there will be cases in which any country will be required to make a last-minute judgment as a responsible member of the international community. I would like to conclude this paper with the hope that it will deepen our understanding of the fact that international law plays a vital role in such actual international politics and policymaking.

Appendix

(Material: Unofficial translation)

Article 1 of the Act on Special Measures against Terrorism (Purpose)

Based upon the fact that the terrorist attacks which took place in the United States on September 11, 2001 (hereinafter referred to as the "terrorist attacks") were regarded as a threat to international peace and security in United Nations Security Council Resolution 1168,

Recalling that the Security Council Resolutions 1267, 1269, 1333 and other Resolutions have condemned the act of international terrorism and requested all States of the United Nations to take appropriate measures to prevent it,

In order that Japan contributes proactively to the efforts of the international community for prevention and eradication of international terrorism,

This Act establishes the following and its purposes are contributing to ensure the peace and security of the international community including Japan.

(1)   Japan's measures, procedures for their implementation, and other necessary matters for making contribution to the activities of the United States and other foreign military forces and other similar organizations (hereinafter referred to as "military forces of foreign countries") that contribute to the achievement of the objectives of the Charter of the United Nations by striving to eliminate the threat posed by terrorist attacks.

(2)   Japan's humanitarian measures, procedures for their implementation, and other necessary matters, based upon the resolution of the United Nations General Assembly, Security Council or the Economic and Social Council, or requested by an organization established by the United Nations General Assembly, a Specialized Agency of the United Nations, or the International Organization for Migration (hereinafter referred to as the "United Nations, etc.").

Notes

1. The White House, "Remarks by the President Upon Arrival at Barksdale Air Force Base, Presidential News and Speeches" (www.whitehouse.gov).
2. Prime Minister's Office, "Prime Minister Junichiro Koizumi announces his statement at the Press Conference Wednesday, September 12, 2001" (www.japan.kantei.go.jp).
3. For general information on Japan's response to the terrorist attacks, see Yachi Shotaro, "9/11 Terrorist Attacks and Japan's Response", *International Affairs, Japan Institute of International Affairs*, No. 503, February 2002, pp. 2-20.
4. Mainichi Interactive, "Simultaneous terrorist attacks in the United States and documents (from the outbreak to noon on the 12th)" (www.mainichi.co.jp).
5. "Clinton Admits Lewinsky Relationship." *The Washington Post*, August 18, 1998.
6. "President Acknowledged Effort to Keep Affair Secret." *The Washington Post*, August 21, 1998.
7. "U.S. Strikes Terrorist-Linked Sites in Afghanistan, Factory in Sudan." *The Washington Post*, August 21, 1998.
8. "Letter dated 20 August 1998 from the permanent representative of the United States of America to the United Nations addressed to the president of the Security Council." UN / S / 1998/780.
9. "The Minutes of the 143rd House of Councilors Budget Committee" No. 3 (August 21, 1998), p.12. "The Minutes of the 143rd House of Councilors Budget Committee" No. 4 (August 24, 1998), p. 2. "The Minutes of the 143rd House of Representatives" No. 6, *Government Bulletin* extra edition, August 25, 1998, p. 9.
10. "The 34th House of Representatives Japan-US Security Treaty Special Committee Minutes" No. 21 (April 20, 1960), p. 26. "The Minutes of the 55th House of Representatives Budget Committee" No. 8 (March 28, 1967), p. 2.
11. Matsuda Takeo, "International terrorism and the right of self-defense: in connection with collective security", *Journal of International Law and Diplomacy*, Vol 101, No. 3, pp.1-20.
12. Onuma Yasuaki (ed), *International law to be read in materials*, Vol. 2, Ed. 2. Toshindo, 2002, p. 69.
13. Mori Tadashi, "Concept of 'self-defense' in the interwar period: Using the cases of protection of foreign nationals in the process of concluding Kellogg-Brian Treaty as material", *Journal of Social Science*, Vol. 53, No. 4, pp. 69-101.

14 US Embassy in Japan, "FBI Most Wanted Terrorists, Network of Terrorism" (www.usembassy.state.gov/tokyo/). Middle East Institute of Japan, "About Osama Bin Laden" (www.meij.or.jp).

15 "The 104th House of Representatives Foreign Affairs Committee Minutes" No. 9 (April 23, 1986), pp. 2-3. "The Minutes of the 104th House of Representatives Security Special Committee" No. 5 (May 19, 1986), pp. 16-17.

16 "Resolution 1214 (1998), Adopted by the Security Council at its 3952nd meeting on December 8, 1998" UN / S / RES / 1214 (1998).

17 "Resolution 1267 (1999), Adopted by the Security Council at its 4051st meeting on October 15, 1999" UN / S / RES / 1267 (1999). "Ministry of Foreign Affairs Notification No. 474", *Government Bulletin* No. 2749, November 12, 1999, pp. 3-4.

18 "Resolution 1333 (2000), Adopted by the Security Council at its 4251st meeting on 19 December 2000" UN / S / RES / 1333 (2000). "Ministry of Foreign Affairs Notification No. 79", *Government Bulletin* No. 3069, March 7, 2001, pp. 3-5.

19 Preamble to "Mutual Cooperation and Security Treaty between Japan and the United States" (1960 Treaty No. 6).

20 "Answer to questions regarding security treaties and defense issues submitted by Member of the House of Representatives Yoshiaki Matsumoto" (April 8, 1969).

21 Onuma Yasuaki (ed), *International law to be read in materials*, Vol. 2, Ed. 2. Toshindo, 2002, p. 7.

22 "Statement by the North Atlantic Council (September 12, 2001)", NATO Press Release, 124 (2001).

23 "Resolution 1368 (2001), Adopted by the Security Council at its 4370th meeting on September 12, 2001, UN/S/RES/1368 (2001), "Ministry of Foreign Affairs Notification, No. 360", *Government Bulletin* extra edition", No. 17, October 12, 2001, p. 1.

24 It is true that the Ministry of Foreign Affairs was relieved by the unanimous response of the international community, but the Treaty Affairs Bureau of the Ministry was most reassured by Professor ONUMA Yasuaki's following comment. "The Charter of the United Nations did not assume a terrorist group as the subject of an armed attack, but a deliberate attack that kills more than 5,000 people would fall into the category of 'an armed attack' in the Charter", "Scholars' Views", Mainichi Shimbun, September 24, 2001.

25 Prime Minister's Office, "About Japan's measures regarding the response to the terrorist attacks in the United States" (www.japan.kantei.go.jp). Prime Minister's Office, "Ministerial Conference on measures against

Terrorism, Prime Minister's Press Conference" (www.japan.kantei.go.jp).

26 For the general picture of the Act, see Mannami Manabu, "About the Act on Special Measures against Terrorism and Activities of Japan based on the Act", *Journal of International Law and Diplomacy*, Vol 101, No. 3, pp. 46-70.

27 The phrase "that contribute to the achievement of the objectives of the Charter of the United Nations" also includes the meaning of guaranteeing the third requirement for exercising the right of self-defense, "exercise of the minimum and necessary force." That is, if the "more" force than necessary to eliminate "infringement of imminent injustice" is used and the situation cannot be understood as a legitimate exercise of the right of self-defense, then such military forces do not "contribute to the achievement of the objectives of the Charter of the United Nations" and is not subject for cooperation under this Act.

28 Letter dated October 7, 2001, from the Permanent Representative of the United States of America to the United Nations addressed to the President of the Security Council, UN/S/2001/946. Letter dated October 7, 2001, from the Charge d'affaires a.i. of the Permanent Mission of the United Kingdom of Great Britain and Northern Ireland to the United Nations addressed to the President of the Security Council, UN/S/2001/947.

29 Press Statement on Terrorist Threats by Security Council President, UN/SC/7167, October 8, 2001.

Chapter II

The End of the War

How World War II ended in Asia

Introduction

Japan announced its acceptance of the Potsdam Declaration on August 15, 1945, and signed "Instrument of Surrender by Japan" on September 2 aboard the United States Navy battleship USS Missouri. This instrument formally proclaimed Japan's unconditional surrender and cease of hostilities; however, it took another 6 years for Japan to achieve peace with the Allied Powers. The "Treaty of Peace with Japan" was signed on September 8, 1951 in San Francisco and came into force on April 28, 1952.

The San Francisco Peace Treaty not only set the peace and the territory, it also included provisions on security, political and economic clauses, and, more than anything, claims and property. Article 14(a)2(I) of the Treaty gave the right to Allied Powers subject to jurisdiction to seize, retain and liquidate or otherwise dispose of all property, rights and interests of Japan and Japanese nationals. Article 16 further stated, "As an expression of its desire to indemnify those members of the armed forces of the Allied Powers who suffered undue hardships while prisoners of war of Japan, Japan will transfer its assets and those of its nationals in countries which were neutral during the war… to the International Committee of the Red Cross…" On the other hand, the Treaty provided for the waiver of all claims of the Allied Powers and their nationals. Article 14(b) wrote, "Except as otherwise provided in the present Treaty, the Allied Powers waive all reparations claims of the Allied Powers, other claims of the Allied

Powers and their nationals arising out of any actions taken by Japan and its nationals in the course of the prosecution of the war, and claims of the Allied Powers for direct military costs of occupation."

However, from the late 1990s to the early 2000s, former US POWs and others filed a series of lawsuits in the United States against Japanese companies seeking monetary compensation for damages caused by Japanese acts during World War II. The reason for these series of litigations was a new California State Law. In July 1999, California enacted this new law, California Code, Code of Civil Procedure, Section 354.6. This State Law allowed any Second World War slave labor victim, forced labor victim or heir of such victim, to bring an action to recover compensation from any entity for whom that labor was performed. The Law also stated that any action brought under this section should not be dismissed for failure to comply with the applicable statute of limitation, if the action is commenced on or before December 31, 2010.[1]

With the enactment of this State Law, former POWs who had engaged in forced labor for Japanese companies during World War II, their bereaved families, etc. filed more than thirty lawsuits against Japanese companies throughout the United States. The plaintiffs in these proceedings included not only the citizens of the parties to the San Francisco Peace Treaty (Allied Powers), like the United States, the United Kingdom, Australia, the Netherlands, New Zealand, and the Philippines, but also the citizens of non-parties to the Peace Treaty like China and South Korea.

The judgement of these proceedings might overturn the conclusion of the Peace Treaty, which had been the foundation of the peace, prosperity and friendship among the nations around the Pacific. Even though the Government of Japan and the United States were not parties to these litigations, there was no option for the two governments to disregard its development.

The United States Government issued several Statements of Interest to the courts saying that despite their deep sympathy with and admiration for the plaintiffs, the United States felt nonetheless compelled to file the Statement of Interest in order to explain that the plaintiffs' claims were barred by international obligations entered into by the United States at the close of World War II.[2]

The Government of Japan also issued two *notes verbales* to the State Department and expressed the views of the Government of Japan on these cases. The first *note verbale* was on the cases against Japanese companies by the nationals of the parties to the San Francisco Peace Treaty. The second *note verbale* was on the cases by the nationals of non-parties to the San Francisco Peace Treaty. The Government of Japan considered the possibility to file statements of interest directly to the US courts; however, the Japanese Government, in the end, avoided such direct involvement into a lawsuit under another country's jurisdiction. Japan preferred a more diplomatic way and expressed that view to the State Department, also with the intention that the defendant companies would quote these views in their pleadings.

As the director of the Legal Affairs Division of the Treaty Bureau at the Ministry of Foreign Affairs of Japan, the author was directly involved in the issuance of the second *note verbale*, that is the cases for the nationals of non-parties to the San Francisco Peace Treaty. Although China was a member of the Potsdam Declaration, Allied Powers did not invite China to the San Francisco Peace Conference. Korea had not been at war with Japan at all. Then how did Japan recover peace with China and how did Japan settle the claim issues with these countries? It was quite a challenge for the author to answer these questions legally and explain them to the US courts. In order to facilitate the full understanding on these issues, the full text of both *notes verbales* are as follows. First appearance of the paper: "The views of the Government of Japan on the lawsuits against Japanese companies alleged to be responsible for forced labor in the World War II era", *The Japanese Annual of International Law*, No. 44, 2001.

The views of the Government of Japan on the lawsuits against Japanese companies alleged to be responsible for forced labor in the World War II era

The Government of Japan transmitted to the Government of the United States the following views in August and November 2000, with regard to the lawsuits against Japanese companies[3] that had been filed in the United States District Court, Northern District of California. These views were quoted by Japanese companies in their pleadings.

The First Note Verbale

> The Views of the Government of Japan on the Lawsuits against Japanese Companies by the Former American Prisoners of War and Others
>
> August 8, 2000

During World War II, Japan caused tremendous damage and suffering to the people of many countries—including the United States—for which actions the Government of Japan has expressed its feelings of deep remorse and its heartfelt apology (please refer to the attached statement of Japanese Prime Minister Murayama in commemoration of the fiftieth anniversary of the end of World War II, which was announced in 1995 and widely circulated, including to all Member States of the United Nations).

In the aftermath of World War II, the settlement of claims arising from the conduct during the war was a diplomatic and political imperative for all affected states. A principal object and purpose of the Treaty of Peace with Japan of September 8, 1951 was the final resolution of war-related claims by the Allied Powers and their nationals against Japan and its nationals. The conclusion of this Treaty enabled Japan to start new relations with other nations as a peaceful, democratic member of the international community.

The Government of Japan fully shares the position of the United States Government that claims of the United States and its nationals (including prisoners of war) against Japan and its nationals arising out of their actions during World War II were settled by the Peace Treaty. The Peace Treaty with Japan was ratified by the United States with overwhelming bipartisan support after thorough deliberation by the United States Senate, and Japan has scrupulously and faithfully fulfilled all of its pecuniary and other obligations thereunder.

Article 14 of the Peace Treaty specifically provides that "the Allied Powers shall waive all … claims of the Allied Powers and their nationals arising out of any actions taken by Japan and its nationals in the course of the prosecution of the war". Under the same Article, Japan acknowledged the United States and other Allied Powers had the right to seize and dispose of Japanese assets that were subject to their jurisdiction. As has been explained by the Government of the United States, out of approximately $90 million of Japanese assets seized by the United States, approximately $20 million were used to take care of claims on behalf of the internees, civilians and prisoners of war under the remedy scheme of the United States (please note that both figures were estimated in 1952 and are not the current value).

With respect to Article 26 of the Peace Treaty, it should be noted that no party to the Peace Treaty has ever invoked that Article in order to obtain the same advantage as provided in peace settlement or war claims settlement that Japan made with other states.

The Government of Japan considers that recent efforts to seek further compensation in United States courts for actions taken by Japanese nationals during World War II would be inconsistent with both the letter and the spirit of the Peace Treaty, and would necessarily be detrimental to bilateral relations between our two countries.

After formally terminating one of history's most destructive wars by concluding the Peace Treaty, Japan and the United States built one of the most constructive and beneficial international partnerships that the world has ever seen—a relationship that is built upon mutual respect, trust and shared values such as democracy, free market economies, the rule of law and respect for fundamental human rights. It would be unfortunate, indeed, if this magnificent edifice were to be adversely affected by efforts to reopen reparations issues that, as both

Japan and the United States agreed, were finally laid to rest over 50 years ago.

The Second Note Verbale

> The Views of the Government of Japan on the Lawsuits against Japanese Companies by the Nationals of the Countries not being a Party to the San Francisco Peace Treaty
>
> November 17, 2000

During the last war, Japan caused tremendous damage and suffering to the people of many countries—including the Chinese people and the people of the Korean Peninsula—for which actions the Government of Japan has expressed its feelings of deep remorse and its heartfelt apology.[4]

In the aftermath of the war, the settlement of claims arising out of the conduct during war was a diplomatic and political imperative for all affected countries. The San Francisco Peace Treaty of September 8, 1951 terminated the state of war between Japan and most of the countries with which Japan was at war, and completely settled all war related claims between Japan and these countries. Under this Peace Treaty, both Japan and these countries waived their own claims and the claims of their nationals.

With respect to the countries not party to the San Francisco Peace Treaty, Japan has settled the issue of claims with these countries through bilateral diplomatic negotiations. The process of the settlements was substantially affected by the cold war in East Asia and the structural changes to the international relationship in this region. In particular, the settlement with China with which Japan was at war, and the settlement with the Republic of Korea which became independent from Japan after the period of annexation, were high on the diplomatic agenda long after the end of the war as issues of utmost importance, difficulty and sensitivity.

China was in a position to be invited to the Peace Conference in San Francisco as one of the Allied Powers. However, neither the Government of the People's Republic of China nor "the National Government of the Republic of China" was invited to the Peace Conference, due to various political and diplomatic developments then taking place, including the establishment of the People's Republic of China in 1949 and the outbreak of the Korean War in 1950. The Allied Powers left Japan to choose which government it would conclude a peace treaty with. After serious consideration, Japan chose "the National Government of the Republic of China, which [had] the seat, voice and vote of China in the United Nations",[5] with the view to making sure that the Senate of the United States should approve the San Francisco Peace Treaty.[6]

Accordingly, Japan signed the "Treaty of Peace Between Japan and the Republic of China" on 28 April 1952: the day on which the San Francisco Peace Treaty came into force. This Treaty terminated the state of war between the two countries, and settled the issue of reparations and other war related claims.

Twenty years later, following U.S. President Nixon's visit to China, the Government of Japan normalized the relationship with the Government of the People's Republic of China by signing the Joint Communique on 29 September 1972. The two governments succeeded in drafting the Joint Communique, a political instrument, in spite of substantial differences in their basic positions. The Government of Japan was of the view that the "Treaty of Peace of 1952" settled all issues related to the war including the issue of reparations claims with China as a state, while the Government of the People's Republic of China asserted that the treaty was from the very beginning null and void. With respect to settlement of claims, the Joint Communique stated, in paragraph 5, that "The Government of the People's Republic of China declares that in the interest of the friendship between the Chinese and the Japanese people, it renounces its demand for war reparation from Japan." This wording is not exactly the same as Article 14(b) of the San Francisco Peace Treaty. This was partly because the Government of Japan held the position that the

"Treaty of Peace of 1952" had settled the issues related to the war with China.

The Joint Communique has been the foundation of reconciliation between Japan and China. The preamble of the "Treaty for Peace and Friendship between Japan and the People's Republic of China," signed on 12 August 1978, confirms that the Joint Communique should be the basis of the relations of peace and friendship between the two countries and that the principles enunciated in the Joint Communique should be strictly observed. Since the Joint Communique was issued in 1972, leaders of the People's Republic of China have expressed the view of the Government by repeatedly stating that they would like to build a positive and peaceful relationship with Japan while recognizing things in the past as they were. "What happened in the past is gone. Hereafter, we should take the attitude of looking forward to the future in building up peaceful relations between our two countries," were the words of Deng Xiaoping, Vice Premier of the People's Republic of China, to Emperor Hirohito in 1978.[7] It is the shared view of the two Governments that the issue of claims related to the war ceased to exist as a bilateral legal issue between Japan and China after the Joint Communique was issued in 1972.

With respect to Korea, which was not at war with Japan, light should be shed from a different angle. The San Francisco Peace Treaty guides the settlement of the question between Japan and the areas that were to be separated from Japan. Article 2 (a) provided that Japan recognizes the independence of Korea, and Article 4 (a) that the disposition of property and claims between Japan and its nationals on the one hand, and the authority and residents in Korea on the other, shall be the subject of a special arrangement between Japan and that authority.

Before entry into force of the San Francisco Peace Treaty, Japan, under the good office of the United States, started negotiations with the Republic of Korea in October 1951 in order to settle issues between the two countries, including the issue of property and claims. Following lengthy and difficult negotiations, the two countries finally reached an agreement in 1965 and signed the "Treaty on Basic Relations Between Japan and the Republic of Korea" and the "Agreement on the Settlement of Problems Concerning Property and Claims and on Economic Cooperation Between Japan and the Republic of Korea." Under the former treaty, the two countries normalized their relations. Under the latter agreement, they confirmed that the problem concerning "property, rights, interests and claims" of the two countries and their nationals, including claims of Korean nationals against Japanese nationals, was settled completely and finally.

The problem concerning property and claims between Japan and North Korea is to be the subject of a special arrangement as stipulated in Article 4 (a) of the San Francisco Peace Treaty, as well. The Government of Japan conducted normalization talks with North Korea eight times from 1991 to 1992 and three times since the resumption of the negotiations in April 2000. The Government of Japan hopes that, through the normalization talks, Japan and North Korea will come to an agreement that will settle this issue.

Thus, Japan has made the utmost effort for the settlement of the issue of claims with countries not being a party to the San Francisco Peace Treaty through bilateral diplomatic negotiations. The Government of the United States has consistently supported this foreign policy of Japan.

Plaintiffs' claims, based on the Code of Civil Procedure of the State of California amended last year (*1999), allegedly relate to the actions taken by non-U.S. nationals against other non-U.S. nationals outside the State of California, even outside the United States, during the last war, more than fifty years ago. Such issues were settled or are being settled through diplomatic negotiations between Japan and the countries concerned, with the support of the Government of the United States.

Permitting plaintiffs' claims will put the courts in the United States in an unwarranted place to inevitably affect relations between the countries concerned, including the bilateral settlement reached after highly political and sensitive negotiations. Such involvement of the courts in the United States could complicate and impede relationships between Japan and those countries as well as the bilateral relationship between the United States and Japan. The Government of Japan is convinced that these issues should not be adjudicated in the courts in the United States.

Epilogue

U.S. District Court in Northern California consolidated most of the cases (Master MDL Docked No. 1347). In that District Court, all the cases filed by former Allied Powers POWs were dismissed in September, 2000, and those cases filed by the nationals of non-parties to the Peace Treaty were dismissed in September, 2001.[8]

Notes

1   California Code, Code of Civil Procedure-CCP §354.6, Current as of January 01, 2019/ Updated by FindLaw Staff (https://www.findlaw. com).

2   In the United States District Court for the Northern District of California San Francisco Division, Statement of Interest of United States of America, Master MDL Docket No. 1347.

3   The defendant Japanese companies include Ishikawajima Harima Heavy Industries Co, Ishihara Sangyo Kaisha, Japan Energy Corp, Kajima Corp, Mitsubishi Corp, Mitsubishi Material Corp, Mitsui & Co, Nippon Sharyo and Nippon Steel Corp.

4   The statement of Japanese Prime Minister Murayama Tomiichi in commemoration of the fiftieth anniversary of the end of World War II, which was announced in 1995 upon Cabinet decision and widely circulated, including to all Member States of the United Nations.

5   Letter from the Prime Minister of Japan (Yoshida) to the Consultant to the Secretary (Dulles), *Foreign Relations of the United States 1951*, Vol. VI, pp.1466-1467. The purpose of this letter was to facilitate the Senate hearing for the ratification of the San Francisco Peace Treaty. Also, Copy of Draft Letter Handed to the Prime Minister of Japan (Yoshida) by the Consultant to the Secretary (Dulles), reprinted in the *Foreign Relations of the United States 1951*, Vol. IV, pp.1445-1447, indicates that this letter was drafted based upon the suggestion of the United States.

6   Memorandum by the Consultant to the Secretary (Dulles) to the Secretary of State, *Foreign Relations of the United States 1951*, Vol. VI, pp. 1467-1470. Also, "Congressional Record, Proceedings and Debates

of the 82nd Congress", Second Session, Senate, Wednesday, January 16, 1952, No. 6.

7   *Xinhua News* (Official News Agency of People's Republic of China, Peking NCNA in English), October 23, 1978. Foreign Broadcast Information Service of the United States of America, Daily Report, People's Republic of China, October 24, 1978.

8   "Kokusaihou no rikoukakuho to kokunaisaibansho niyoru kokusaihou no tekiyou-iwayuru 'beikokuPOWsoshou' womegutte" ["Ensuring the performance of international law and applying international law by domestic courts; Over the so-called "US POW proceedings"], KOMATSU Ichiro, *Kokusaifunsou no tayouka to houtekishori* ["Diversification of international disputes and legal processing"], Shinzansha, pp. 209-241.

Chapter III

The Remnants of War: Chemical Weapon

Poisonous Gas Accident in Qiqihar City, Heilongjiang Province

Introduction

On August 9, 2003, a commemorative reception was held at the Great Hall of the People to celebrate the 25th anniversary of the conclusion of the Japan-China Peace and Friendship Treaty in Beijing, China. Chief Cabinet Secretary Yasuo Fukuda visited China from Japan to attend the reception with the Chairman of the Standing Committee of the National People's Congress Wu Bangguo. On the same day, Chief Cabinet Secretary Fukuda met with President Hu Jintao and Chairman Wu Bangguo, and on the following day, he met with Prime Minister Wen Jiabao. At this meeting, Prime Minister Wen called for the Japanese side to take appropriate measures in the case where more than 30 people were injured by the abandoned chemical weapons of the former Japanese army in Qiqihar City, Heilongjiang Province, China. In response to this statement, Chief Cabinet Secretary Fukuda replied that Japanese experts were currently investigating the incident and if the facts became clear, the Japanese Government would take appropriate measures.[1]

On October 20, the Japan-China summit meeting was held in Bangkok, Thailand. In this meeting, about two months after the meeting in Beijing, President Hu Jintao told Prime Minister Junichiro Koizumi that the response to this incident was agreed between the office levels of both countries.[2]

In this paper, I would like to clarify how the parties concerned in both countries acted in response to an unprecedented incident for both Japan and China, namely the occurrence of large-scale damage caused by the abandoned chemical weapons of the former Japanese Army, and what kind of understanding had brought the two sides to the final solution on this matter. The author was involved in the response to the accident and the discussions with the Chinese side as the director of the China Division, Asian and Oceanian Affairs Bureau of the Ministry of Foreign Affairs of Japan at the time of the accident. However, the views expressed in this paper do not represent the views of the government or the Ministry of Foreign Affairs, except for direct citations such as parliamentary responses and external announcements.

First appearance of the paper: "Poisonous gas accident in Qiqihar City, Heilongjiang Province", Yushindo-kobunsha "Agenda for International Law in the 21st Century: Professor Ando Nisuke Jubilee Publishing", July 2006.

1. Occurrence of an accident[3]

(1) First site, Beijiang Garden construction site

Around 4:00 am on August 4, 2003, five rusty drums were dug out from the ground a little over two meters underground at the foundation construction site of Beijiang Garden, Airport Road, Longsha District, Qiqihar City, Heilongjiang Province, China. One of the drums lying on the construction site had already been completely damaged, the liquid inside had flowed out to the surroundings, and some of the other drums were covered with iron rust and had holes. The drums were removed to the vicinity of the site by construction machinery and sold to a waste collection company around 9:00 am on the same day. At this first site in Beijiang Garden, 16 people developed symptoms of poisoning on their skin, respiratory organs, and eyes.

(2) Second site, Longsha District Tie'nan Waste Collection Station

The waste collection company carried the sold drums to the Tie'nan Waste Collection Station. From the appearance of the damaged drum, it looked like the lid was made of copper, the outer wall of the drum was iron, and the inner wall was lead. Since the collection prices for iron, copper, and lead are different, the waste collection company started dismantling the drums near the station. First they opened the copper lid of the drum, which was still in its original shape, and weighed it. At that time, the people around said that a strong mustard odor had spilled out. The four other drums, which had remained in their original form, were to be shipped to Daqing City, and were ready for transport at 1:00 pm. Meanwhile, the dismantling of the damaged drum continued, and the inner and outer walls were separated by 3:00 pm. The two waste collectors engaged in this dismantling work had the most severe symptoms, and were taken to the hospital around 6:00 pm, with headache and vomiting. This was reported to the public security authority at 8:00 pm with the result that the four drums being transported to Daqing City were sent back to Qiqihar City around 10:00 pm. In the meantime at the waste collection station, six people developed symptoms of poisoning.

(3) Third site, Xinjiang 2nd Street Private House

In Qiqihar city it had been raining continuously, and private houses in Xinjiang 2nd Street were suffering from flooding. On August 4, to protect their houses against flooding, the head of one family with his four neighbors went to the construction site of Beijiang Garden, received surplus soil excavated there, and carried it to the front door of his house. The five of them then went out to eat, but at that time also noticed that each other's eyes were red. The owner of the house started vomiting at home at 8 pm and was taken to the hospital. His family told the hospital that he might have drunk fake liquor, and without receiving sufficient medical treatment at the hospital he went back home. On the morning of the next day, August 5, it was found that his four neighbors also had similar symptoms. In addition, three children who had been playing with the soil that had been brought in also showed symptoms of poisoning. Their mothers brought the soil to the Qiqihar City Epidemic Prevention Station and the city's Environmental Protection Center and asked for an appraisal, but neither institution had the ability to chemically inspect earth and sand. As it was suspected that the accident was caused by abandoned chemical weapons of the former Japanese Army, a cadre of the Environmental Protection Center visited the city government's Production Safety Supervision Bureau together with two of the mothers. Since the situation was similar to the onset at the Beijiang Garden construction site, those people who had developed symptoms of poisoning were transferred to the Liberation Army 203 Hospital.

(4) Fourth site, Fengtun Chemical Factory

The four drums that had been sent back to Qiqihar City were brought to the Fengtun Chemical Factory site in Qiqihar City. The night watchman at the factory, who looked into the drums at the time of delivery, also developed symptoms and was transferred to the Liberation Army 203 Hospital.

(5) Emergency measures taken by Chinese Authority

All of the above people who developed symptoms of poisoning were examined and treated at the Liberation Army 203 Hospital from August 4 to 9. The hospital invited experts from Liberation Army 307 Hospital, Shenyang Military Medical Research Institute, and Liberation Army 321 Hospital to make a diagnosis, and as a result, they identified 31 mustard gas poisoning patients. During this time, Qiqihar City requested support from the People's Liberation Army, and a high-ranking engineer from the Shenyang Military Region's Office, specializing in chemical weapons abandoned by former Japanese troops, rushed to the site. He assessed the appearance of the drums and conducted chemical analysis. He determined that the poison was indeed an abandoned chemical weapon (mustard gas) of the former Japanese troops. On August 6, officials from the Chinese Foreign Ministry's Office working on the issue of abandoned chemical weapons by former Japanese troops, the Ministry of National Defense's Foreign Affairs Office, the PLA General Staff Department, Shenyang Military Region, etc. arrived in Qiqihar City, and they started the relief activities along with on-site appraisals. On August 8, simple packaging of the five drums was carried out under the arrangement of the local government and the PLA. On August

9, Chinese authorities locked up Beijiang Garden construction site, Tie'nan waste collection station, Xinjiang 2nd Street residential area, and Fengtun chemical factory site, together with Qiqihar City No. 5 Junior High School and Nan'yuan Automobile Castle which were contaminated by the transportation of construction surplus soil. In total, 10 sites and vehicles were locked up, and confirmation, appraisal, inspection, disinfection, soil removal, etc. of residual contaminants were carried out.

(6) Representation to Japan

On the afternoon of August 8, while relief activities were continuing in Qiqihar City, a representation was made to the Japanese side in Beijing based on the results of the local appraisal. It was four days after the accident that the Director-General of Asia department of Ministry of Foreign Affairs, Fu Ying, urgently invited the Japanese embassy minister in Beijing to report the occurrence of the incident and lodged representation.[4]

2. The issue of Abandoned Chemical Weapons in China (Part 1 Entering into force of the Chemical Weapon Convention)

(1) Abandoned chemical weapons of the former Japanese Army

In order to discuss the Japanese government's response to this accident, it is necessary to unravel the history of the issue of abandoned chemical weapons in China. Development and large scale production of chemical weapons, commonly referred to as poisonous gas weapons, had started around World War I. Recognizing that chemical weapons were successful in that war, the former Japanese army began research and development of chemical weapons around 1924, and in 1929 started manufacturing chemicals at Tadanoumi Weapons Factory, Ohkunoshima in the Seto Inland Sea. In 1937, full-scale production of chemical shells began at Sone Weapons Factory in Kokura City, Fukuoka Prefecture, and it is said that production continued until the war situation deteriorated around 1945. Those chemical weapons produced in Japan were sent by ship from ports in Kitakyu-shu and the Hokuriku region to logistics bases in China.[5] Chemical agents which had been confirmed to be developed and owned by the former Japanese Army include blister agents (yellow agents, mustard and lewisite), vomiting agents (red agents, diphenylcyanoarsine, etc.), tear gas agents (green agents, chloroacetophenone), choking agents (blue agents, fosgen), and blood agents (brown agents, hydrogen cyanarsine), etc.[6]

(2) Manifestation of the issue of abandoned chemical weapons in China

The issue of abandoned chemical weapons in China was put on the agenda in the process of treaty negotiations aimed at the abolition of chemical weapons, which began in the latter half of the 1980s.[7] The use of chemical weapons by the Iraqi army in the Iran-Iraq War and the collapse of the Cold War structure triggered the establishment of the Weapons Prohibition Special Committee at the Conference on Disarmament in Geneva (later the Conference on Disarmament). This Special Committee started a serious negotiation aiming at a treaty, which would not only prohibit the use of chemical weapons but also their development, production and storage, and stipulate their destruction.[8] In the process of negotiations to formulate the treaty, the issues of chemical weapons abandoned by a foreign coun-try and the destruction of those weapons also became an important agenda item. In 1990, the Chinese government requested the cooper-ation of the Japanese government on the issue of chemical weapons that the former Japanese army allegedly abandoned in China. In February 1992, the Chinese government submitted a report to the Conference on Disarmament in Geneva, where the negotiation on the Chemical Weapon Convention was ongoing, and argued that two million former Japanese military chemical weapons had been aban-doned in China.[9]

(3) Entry into force of the Chemical Weapon Convention

At the time of the end of the Cold War and with the frequent oc-currence of regional conflicts, strengthening the non-proliferation system of weapons of mass destruction and missiles was an urgent issue for the international community. The Japanese government was also committed to making further efforts to lead the negotiation of the Chemical Weapon Convention to an early conclusion.[10] Regarding the issue of abandoned chemical weapons in China, which came to light in the process of the negotiations, the Ministry of Foreign Affairs of Japan had taken the lead in conducting a field survey jointly with China and with the cooperation of the Defense Agency and experts of the private sector since 1991.[11]

The negotiations on the convention in Geneva were settled by obliging the parties who had abandoned chemical weapons within the territory of other parties to destroy the abandoned chemical weapons. United Nations Conference on Disarmament adopted the Chemical Weapon Convention, and Japan signed the Convention at the Paris signing ceremony in January 1993.[12]

Regarding the issue of abandoned chemical weapons in China before the Convention came into force, it was the policy of the Japanese government to conduct field surveys on the actual situation of abandoned chemical weapons and grasp the facts first and to discuss the specific treatment method with the Chinese side based upon the spirit of the Japan-China Joint Communique, the Japan-China Peace and Friendship Treaty, and the Chemical Weapons Convention.[13] The Japanese government also held its legal position that the issue of claims related to the previous war with China did not exist after the issuance of the Japan-China Joint Communique in 1972.

If unexploded ordnance is found between nations that have legally settled the issue of claims related to war, it is usually the responsibility of the country where the unexploded ordnance is found. For example, on July 10, 2005, at the time of writing this article, an evacuation advisory was issued to about 3100 households and about 7000 people had evacuated to schools and public halls in Nishitokyo City, Tokyo. While the residents were temporarily evacuated, a large-scale unexploded bomb operation was carried out. It was the processing of the so-called one-ton bomb dropped by the U.S. military at the time of World War II and the operation was carried out by the Ground Self-Defense Force of Japan.[14]

However, the Japanese government decided to take a more in-depth response to the issue of abandoned chemical weapons in China since 1991. It considered it appropriate to first grasp the facts and to proceed with discussions with the Chinese side on the specific treatment method, because it was predicted that providing all the funds, technology, experts, facilities and other resources necessary for their destruction would be obligated after the coming into force of the Chemical Weapons Convention.[15]

Coordination with the Chinese side on the issue of abandoned chemical weapons in China was carried to a higher stage in April 1997 when the two governments established the Japan-China collaborative work group, following a total of four intergovernmental consultations held between January 1991 and December 1996.[16] On the other hand, the field surveys had also been carried out with the cooperation of the Chinese side. Site visits were conducted in Harbaling, Dunhua District. Jilin Province and Shijiazhuang District, Hebei Province in June 1991, and in Nanjing City, Jiangsu Province in June 1992.[17] Based on the knowledge gained through such field visits, the technical studies in Japan, and the common understanding obtained through discussions with the Chinese side on the process of destruction of abandoned chemical weapons, the Japanese government began field surveys, which actually involved the sealing of chemical weapons and poisonous agents in 1995. The first such field survey was conducted in Hangzhou City, Zhejiang Province, Chuzhou City, Anhui Province and Nanjing City, Jiangsu Province from February to March of that year. The second field survey was conducted in Harbaling, Dunhua District, Jilin Province and Meihekou, Liaoyuan City, Jilin Province in May and June of that year and the third survey was conducted in September of the same year in Shenyang City, Liaoning Province, Jilin City, Jilin Province, and Harbin City, Heilongjiang Province.[18] This field survey activity of sealing, transferring, and storing abandoned chemical weapons by a joint team of Japan and China has been carried out throughout China since then, and is still ongoing.

In Japan, the Matsumoto sarin attack incident occurred in June 1994 and the subway sarin attack in Tokyo occurred in March 1995. These two incidents raised public awareness on the issue of chemical weapons, and the Japanese Diet approved the conclusion of the Chemical Weapons Convention in April 1995. Japan ratified the Convention in September of the same year and China ratified it in April 1997. The Chemical Weapons Convention entered into force on April 29, 1997.[19]

3. The Japanese government's responses to the incident

(1) August 8: Dispatch of Japanese personnel

Upon receiving a report from the Chinese side regarding the poisonous gas accident in Qiqihar City, the government of Japan immediately started to dispatch Japanese personnel to the site to investigate the facts as soon as possible. This was the first time that the Japanese government received notification of the damage to the Chinese people caused by the abandoned chemical weapons. There was an urgent need for the Japanese side to independently assess the drums and confirm the cause of this unprecedented accident of more than 30 poisoned patients, in order to consider the government's response. On August 8 when the Ministry of Foreign Affairs of China made representations in Beijing, there was a Japanese investigation team who was conducting the 25th Field Survey on Abandoned Chemical Weapons in China, working in Ning'an City, Mudanjiang District, Heilongjiang Province. The Government of Japan decided to dispatch four members (Ministry of Foreign Affairs, Cabinet Office and private experts) from this investigation team to Qiqihar city as quickly as possible. The four people left Mudanjiang District that afternoon together with a Chinese Foreign Ministry staff member, who was engaged in the field survey activity. They arrived in Qiqihar City before dawn on the 9th.[20]

(2) August 9 and 10: field survey

On August 9 and 10, the Japanese investigation team, who had arrived in Qiqihar City, listened to the explanations from the Qiqihar city authorities about the situation of the occurred accident, the progress, the damage, etc. They also listened to the explanations from

Chinese experts and visited the site where the drums were found. They also appraised the drums, which had been kept in temporary storage. In the appraisal, they unwrapped the drums that had already been packed by the Chinese side, and scrutinized the appearance, detailed structure, and dimensions of the container while comparing it with the materials of the former Japanese military weapons. They also inspected the contents. As a result, they found and reported to the Japanese government that these drums were judged to be abandoned chemical weapons (military containers filled with yellow agents) of the former Japanese army. During their stay in Qiqihar City, the Japanese investigation team also visited the Liberation Army 203 Hospital to see patients who had been hospitalized due to poisoning.[21]

On August 9 and 10, when the Japanese investigation team was engaged in a field survey in Qiqihar city, a reception was held in Beijing to celebrate the 25th anniversary of the conclusion of the Japan-China Peace and Friendship Treaty. Between Chief Cabinet Secretary Fukuda who attended this commemoration from Japan and Chinese officials, a series of talks were held as mentioned in the introduction.

(3) August 11: Japan-China Foreign Ministers' Meeting (Tokyo)

On August 11, three days after the representation in Beijing, a Japan-China Foreign Ministers' Meeting was held in Tokyo between Foreign Minister Li Zhaoxing, who was visiting Japan for the first time after taking office as the Foreign Minister of China, and Foreign Minister of Japan, Yoriko Kawaguchi. At the meeting, ahead of the first meeting of the Six-Party Talks, which would be held in Beijing at the end of the same month, in-depth exchanges took place on the situation in North Korea, including the pending issues between Japan and North Korea. They also had a wide ranging discussion over the bilateral relations which had just been celebrated with the 25th Anniversary of the Peace and Friendship Treaty. During the meeting, Foreign Minister Kawaguchi told Minister Li that she had received a report from a Japanese expert team on an accident involving the abandoned chemical weapons of the former Japanese Army in Qiqihar City, Heilongjiang Province, China. She also stated that after confirming the facts, Japan would like to deal with the accident in good faith under close cooperation with the Chinese side.[22]

(4) August 12: Press Secretary's Statement and the second representation

After scrutinizing the report of the field survey conducted in Qiqihar City, the Japanese government confirmed that the drum that caused the accident was an abandoned chemical weapon of the former Japanese army. On August 12, the Ministry of Foreign Affairs issued a statement by the Press Secretary and expressed that the Government of Japan considered such an accident extremely regrettable and expressed its heartfelt sympathy to the victims, while feeling strong compassion for them.[23] The statement reiterated that, to prevent such damage in the future, it was the intention of the Government of Japan to deal with dangerous abandoned chemical weapons as soon as possible, and to dispose of them properly as obligated by the Chemical Weapons Convention. The statement also clarified the Government of Japan's position to deal with the accident in good faith while cooperating closely with the Chinese side.

On the same day in Beijing, Vice Foreign Minister of China Wang Yi called in Japanese Ambassador Koreshige Anami and lodged the second representation on the accident. In the representation it was revealed that the number of local poisoned patients had reached more than 40, among them 36 patients were hospitalized, and 10 were seriously ill.[24]

That afternoon, the author was at the tourist spot Lake Ashi in Kanagawa Prefecture, as I was accompanying Chinese Foreign Minister Li Zhaoxing on a visit to Hakone after finishing the busy Tokyo schedule. During the visit, Mt. Fuji could not be seen due to the summer fog on the day, but Minister Li invited the staff of the Chinese Embassy in Tokyo to actively exchange opinions. Then I saw Mme. Fu Ying, Director-General of Asian affairs of the Foreign Ministry of China, on the deck looking into the lake with a serious look. She told me that, since the start of Mr. Li's visit to Japan, she had been in contact with the home government every day about the progress of the poisonous gas accident in Qiqihar City. According to her, the reported condition of the hospitalized patients was serious. Since it was an accident on an unprecedented scale in China, concerns of domestic stakeholders were extremely strong, and the treatment of mustard gas poisoning had not been perfect in China. She also told the author that at the meeting on that morning between Minister Li and the Secretary Generals of three ruling parties of Japan they had discussed the treatment of the victims of the accident. After the field survey, grasping the facts and issuance of the Press Secretary's Statement, Mme. Fu Ying's story gave a suggestion to the Government of Japan for considering their further response to the accident. The work to dispatch medical specialists to the site began on the same day.

(5) August 13 and 14: Examination within the Japanese government

In China, a great deal of news had been reported every day since August 8 when the Japanese side was notified of the accident. On August 13, the *People's Daily* published four articles including an article about the second representation to the Japanese side on the previous day and reports from the field.[25] The *Global Times* on the same day revealed the existence of strong emotions in China, posting an article that raised the issue of the lack of coverage in Japan regarding the accident ("Poisonous agent incident, few reports in the Japanese media").[26]

Under such circumstances, the matters that the Japanese government should deal with were obvious.

First, prevent further damage from spreading locally. Specifically, from the report of the Japanese investigation team that arrived at the site on August 9, the day after the representation, it was found that the storage condition of the drum-shaped container that triggered this accident was not perfect, and it was highly likely that leaking chemical agent would contaminate the inside of the building. In order to prevent the spread of such contamination and ensure safety during storage, it was necessary to dispatch an expert to the site again and perform sealed packaging (simple packaging) with aluminum laminate. A team of Japanese experts (composed of the Ministry of Foreign Affairs, the Cabinet Office, and six private experts) to carry out this work arrived at the site on August 14.[27]

Second, take all possible measures to treat the victims. It was hoped that sharing the knowledge about the treatment of the poisoning with the Chinese side could be useful for treatment of those more than 40 patients who had suffered from the chemical weapons of the former Japanese army, which had not lost its toxicity 58 years after the war. Contacts with the people concerned started. The initial expectation of the Ministry of Foreign Affairs was to seek cooperation from the Self Defense Forces related departments. However, the response from the Defense side was that the Self Defense Forces, which was established after the war, had no experience in actually treating the damage caused by chemical weapons, and the knowledge level of SDF was no better than the Peoples Liberation Army of China. Under these circumstances, the Cabinet Office for Destruction of Abandoned Chemical Weapons made suggestions to the Ministry of Foreign Affairs about two medical research institutes: Tokyo Women's Medical University and Kitasato University Hospital. In contact with Tokyo Women's Medical University, the Foreign Ministry had the opportunity to consult with an expert who participated in an international research team to verify the use of chemical weapons in the Iran-Iraq War, but it turned out that the expert actually had not treated the victims of chemical weapons and he did not have his own clinical findings. As a result, Kitasato University Hospital became the last resort for the Foreign Ministry. At Kitasato University Hospital, Dr. Yasushi Asari (Intensive Care Unit Chief, K.U.H.) actually had treated the victims of a poison gas accident that had occurred at the site of the former Sagami Navy Factory in Samukawa-cho, Koza-gun, Kanagawa Prefecture in September 2002.[28] Although the request was sudden and one-sided in this midsummer vacation season from the Foreign Ministry to visit Qiqihar City to see more than 40 victims of chemical weapons accidents and to exchange opinions with the Chinese medical team, Dr. Asari agreed to go. He also called upon Dr. Yoshihiro Yamaguchi (Associate Professor, Kyorin University), a burns specialist to deal with the characteristic symptoms (erosion) of mustard gas and Lewisite poisoning, and Dr. Masayasu Arai (Lecturer, Kitasato University), a specialist in emergency medical care, to join. The team of medical experts was then set up.

(6) From August 15 to 18: Dispatch of the medical expert team and completion of sealed packaging

On August 15, the sealing and packaging process of drum-shaped containers was successfully carried out in Qiqihar City through joint work between Japan and China. Around the same time, a small departure ceremony for the team of seven medical experts (Dr. Asari, Dr. Yamaguchi, Dr. Arai, the Ministry of Foreign Affairs, Cabinet Office and a private expert) was held at Narita Airport. After the accident, feelings toward Japan in Qiqihar City had deteriorated significantly, and when the Japanese investigation team who arrived at the site the day after the notification visited the PLA 203 Hospital, the families of the inpatients got excited and the hospital room was on the brink of disorder. At the departure ceremony, the participants shared information about the local atmosphere and the Chinese Government's stance to ensure the safety of the medical expert team. All of them confirmed the common wish of the victims for early recovery.

On the afternoon of August 16, the medical experts' team arrived at the Liberation Army's 203 Hospital. They listened to the Chinese medical team about the patients' current medical condition, treatment progress, etc., and then went around the hospital rooms of all 41 inpatients and consulted with Chinese doctors. On the following day, August 17, they interviewed Chinese doctors again on the treatment methods at the 203 Hospital, and in that afternoon held a meeting between the two medical teams for exchange of opinions and summarization.[29] During this period, the 203 Hospital suspended outpatient reception and patient visits, ensuring an environment in which the Japanese medical team could concentrate on medical examinations. The Chinese doctors, who initially showed a firm attitude on the afternoon of the 16th, increased their trust in the Japanese doctors by exchanging expert opinions on the medical condition, progress, and treatment policy of each patient. At the final meeting on August 17, the Chinese doctors listened enthusiastically to the Japanese team's introduction with slides of treatment cases in Samukawa-cho, Kanagawa Prefecture, and made a series of remarks asking for frank advice. The Chinese side's concern was focused on the future treatment policy for one serious patient (a waste collector who dismantled the drum can-shaped container at the Tie'nan Waste Collection Station), and the Japanese side evaluated that the Chinese doctors' treatment so far had been highly effective and gave specific advice from their respective specialized viewpoints.

The Chinese media also showed great interest in the activities of the Japanese medical expert team, in newspapers and from TV coverage. Chinese authorities also actively responded, such as allowing coverage in the military hospital. The activities of this medical expert team let them accurately grasp the medical condition of the victims, and from the Chinese medical team they received a positive evaluation on their medical advice. Also through the Chinese media, Japan's sincerity regarding this accident was shown to local residents and Chinese citizens.[30]

(7) August 21: The death of the seriously ill patient

On August 21, one serious patient who had been continuing treatment at the PLA 203 Hospital Intensive Care Unit died. On the following day, August 22, in Beijing, Vice Foreign Minister Wang Yi called in Japanese Ambassador Koreshige Anami to the Ministry of Foreign Affairs and lodged a new representation. On the same day, Ministry of Foreign Affairs of Japan issued another statement by the Press Secretary which expressed the Government's heartfelt condolences to the family of the victim.[31]

4. The issue of Abandoned Chemical Weapons in China (Part 2 After entering into force of the Chemical Weapon Convention)

(1) Establishing an organization within the Japanese government

Following the entry into force of the Chemical Weapons Convention in April 1997, Japan's first effort in relation to the issue of abandoned chemical weapons in China was the establishment of a system within the government to tackle this matter. There were many unprecedented subjects to deal with, including many issues that cannot be addressed by a single ministry, such as ensuring consistency with the Chemical Weapons Convention, impacting Japan-China relations, confirming the reliability of new technologies, and assessing the impact on the environment, etc. In order to deal with the situation as a whole, the Japanese government established the Abandoned Chemical Weapons Destruction Measures Liaison and Coordination Conference in the Cabinet in August 1997, and established the Abandoned Chemical Weapons Destruction Measures Office in the Cabinet Secretariat in October of the same year. Furthermore, in April 1999, the Prime Minister's Office established the Abandoned Chemical Weapons Office as a division in charge of destruction of abandoned chemical weapons. Since the central government reform in 2001, the Office has belonged to the Cabinet Office.[32]

(2) Signing of the Memorandum of Understanding between Japan and China

Through the Japan-China joint field survey and discussions under the joint working group, which had started before the entering into force of the Chemical Weapons Convention, the two governments reached a common understanding on the basic framework of the destruction of abandoned chemical weapons (ACWs) in China. The signing of the Memorandum of Understanding on the Destruction of ACWs in China took place in Beijing on July 30, 1999, between Ambassador Sakutaro Tanino and Mr. Wang Yi, Assistant Minister of the Ministry of Foreign Affairs of China.

In the Memorandum, the Government of Japan confirmed that Japan will fulfill the obligation under the Chemical Weapons Convention for destruction of the ACWs and, in accordance with the relevant provisions of the Verification Annex of the Convention, will provide all necessary financial, technical, expert, facility as well as other resources for the purpose of destroying the ACWs. Upon the confirmation by the Japanese Government to comply with relevant Chinese laws in conducting the destruction operation, the Government of China also agreed that the destruction operation would be carried out inside its territory.

With the signing and issuance of this Memorandum, the basic framework for destruction of ACWs was established, in which the destruction facilities would be constructed in China and the operation would be carried out without transporting the ACWs of the former Japanese Army outside China. The two Governments also agreed on the key scheme to settle issues including the location of the destruction facilities and their construction, environmental standards, and specific destruction technology, etc. through discussions at joint working groups.[33]

(3) Excavation / recovery operation in Bei'an City, Heilongjiang Province

The destruction process of abandoned chemical weapons is roughly divided into three processes: exploration, excavation/recovery, and actual destruction. Of these, the process of exploring the burial area (horizontal extent and depth) of chemical weapons and excavating and recovering the chemical weapons buried in the ground can be called the pre-destruction stage. The chemical weapons of the former Japanese Army contain not only chemical agents but also explosives, which have been buried in large quantities, so careful planning and preparation including explosion risk management are required even at the excavation and recovery stage. The largest target was an estimated 300,000 to 400,000 abandoned chemical weapons buried in Harbaling. How to safely carry out excavation and recovery there, how to establish remote control technology to minimize injuries from chemical agents and risk of shell explosion, are still ongoing discussions between Japan and China.

On the other hand, the two Governments started excavation and recovery projects in areas other than Harbaling. In September 2000, they carried out the first large-scale excavation and recovery operation in Bei'an City, Heilongjiang Province.[34]

It was estimated that 1,500 shells, including about 500 chemical weapons, had been buried in the city close to the residential area, and the Japanese and Chinese sides shared the view that an early excavation and recovery operation was necessary. At the excavation site, a protective dome with a diameter of 16 meters and a height of 9 meters was constructed to prevent the leakage of toxic gas during work and to minimize the damage in the event of an accident. More than 800 residents were temporarily evacuated during the operation period, from September 13 to 27, 2000. For the actual excavation and recovery operation, about 70 public and private officials and experts, including Self Defense Forces personnel participated from the Japanese side and worked in collaboration with more than 150 experts and workers of the Chinese side. This excavation and recovery operation in Bei'an City became the first tangible major work of the destruction of ACWs in China by Japan, and it succeeded in collecting 3080 shells including 897 chemical shells (mainly yellow agent) which exceeded the initial estimation.

(4) Subsequent excavation / recovery operations

The safe excavation and recovery of chemical weapons in Bei'an City, Heilongjiang Province gave great confidence to the people concerned in both countries. The two Governments proceeded with excavation and recovery operations at abandoned chemical weapons burial sites scattered throughout China:[35]

2001, Huanghuzishan, Nanjing City, Jiangsu Province. The abandoned chemical weapons buried there had been discovered in 1998 during urban development work. The excavation and recovery work, which had been originally planned to take about two weeks as in Bei'an City, was significantly extended due to the generation of spring water and the collection of a large amount of debris. The work lasted for 32 days from November to December 2001. At this site, 9419 shells were collected, centering on the red cylinders and the green cylinders.

September 2002, Sunwu County, Heilongjiang Province. In Sunwu County, which is located along the border between China and Russia, about 150 kilometers north of Bei'an, local residents' desire for early excavation and recovery had been rising since the successful implementation of Bei'an's operation. The work in the prefecture lasted for three weeks, and a total of 377 shells, including red shells, yellow shells and toxic smoke bombs, and four drum-shaped containers believed to contain chemical agents were recovered.

September 2003, Shijiazhuang City, Hebei Province. Fifty-one shells were collected, mainly yellow shells, one of which was estimated to be a blue-white shell, phosgene.

June 2004, Ang'angxi District, Qiqihar City, Heilongjiang Province. Since the abandoned chemical weapons of the former Japanese army were discovered in the garden of a private house in May, 2004, urgent excavation and a recovery operation was carried out; 542 shells were recovered, mainly red shells.

August 2004, Xinyang City, Henan Province. Excavated and recovered 73 shells centering on red shells.

September 2004, Ning'an, Mudanjiang City, Heilongjiang Province. Recovered 89 abandoned chemical weapons (including 22 unknown ammunition). From this excavation site, more than 2000 bullets, land mines, grenades, rifle bullets, etc. were excavated in a mixed manner, and these were handed over to the Chinese side.

July 2005, Guangzhou City, Guangdong Province. Excavated and recovered 13 shells centering on red shells.

September 2005, Yi'chun City, Heilongjiang Province. Excavated and recovered 281 shells centering on red shells and yellow shells.

(5) Current status of the issue of abandoned chemical weapons in China

While excavation and recovery operations have been promoted in various parts of China, technical studies by experts from both Japan and China have also progressed, and the eighth meeting of the Japan-China Joint Working Group was held in Tokyo in April 2004. At the meeting, the construction site of the actual destruction facility for abandoned chemical weapons was decided. The experts had narrowed it down to two possible locations. Then the Japanese side proceeded with the study of facility layout plans, shell transportation methods, etc., and the Chinese side conducted geological surveys and environmental surveys of these candidate sites. After these studies, the two sides jointly decided to construct the destruction facility about 4 km west of the shell burial site in the Harbaling district.[36]

Regarding the processing technology for abandoned chemical weapons, it was decided at the seventh meeting of the Japan-China

Joint Working Group of the previous year that incineration would be used as the destruction technology, main plant processing technology, for standard yellow shells and red shells. At the eighth meeting of the Joint Working Group, it was also decided that incineration would be the destruction technology, as sub-plant processing technology for other objects, like non-standard yellow shells and red shells, other types of chemical shells, toxic smoke cylinders, chemical agents in drum-shaped containers, etc. In addition, it was agreed that experts of both countries would examine the destruction technology for the objects stored in various parts of China and efforts would be made to reach a consensus at an early stage.

With the decision on the actual destruction technology and the construction site of the processing facility, the issue of abandoned chemical weapons in China had taken a big step toward its final solution. At the stage of writing this paper, the Chinese government's approval for the construction of a large-scale facility in Harbaling awaits, and in order to start logging and constructing in 2005, studies from technical, safety and institutional aspects are underway in both Japan and China.

5. Japan-China talks and final settlement

Regarding the issue of the Qiqihar poisonous gas accident, high-level exchanges had been held between the two governments since September 2003, and official-level consultation had been held three times in Beijing. On October 19, a document between the Japanese and Chinese governments confirmed the final settlement.

(1) High-level exchanges between Japan and China

a) Visit to Japan by Wu Bangguo, Chairman of the National People's Congress (September 4 to 10)

The 25th Anniversary Reception of the Japan-China Peace and Friendship Treaty was held at the Akasaka Prince Hotel in Tokyo on September 5. In order to attend this celebration, Chairman of the Standing Committee of the National People's Congress, Wu Bangguo (Member of the Standing Committee of the Central Political Bureau of the Communist Party of China, second in party ranking) visited Japan at the invitation of both Houses of Parliament. Prior to attending the reception, Chairman Wu Bangguo met with Chairman of the House of Representatives Watanuki and Chairman of the House of Councilors Kurata, and visited the Prime Minister's office to meet with Prime Minister Koizumi. At every meeting, Chairman Wu raised the issue of the Qiqihar poisonous gas accident. Prime Minister Koizumi expressed his condolences to the victim who died in the accident and stated that the Japanese Government regretted the occurrence of such an accident and would like to respond in good faith, while closely cooperating with the Chinese side.[37]

b) Japan-China Foreign Ministers' Meeting at the United Nations General Assembly (September 24, in New York)

Foreign Minister Kawaguchi from Japan attended the 58th UN General Assembly. She took up the issue of the abduction of Japanese citizens by North Korea for the first time in the General Debate at the General Assembly, and emphasized the importance of working together as an international community to deal with the spread of weapons of mass destruction and the threat of terrorism. Minister Kawaguchi attended the UN General Assembly on a hectic schedule of one night and two days, but during the limited time in New York, the Japan-China Foreign Ministers' Meeting was held on the morning of the September 24. At the meeting, Foreign Minister Li Zhaoxing raised the issue. He said that while he was told that the Japanese Government would like to respond in good faith to the Qiqihar poisonous gas accident, it is hoped that the case would be dealt with promptly to resolve the matter. Foreign Minister Kawaguchi stated that the Government of Japan would like to respond promptly to this matter and would like to continue to respond in good faith.[38]

c) Japan-China Prime Ministers' Meeting (October 7, in Bali)

The 2003 ASEAN + Japan-China-Korea Summit was held in Bali, Indonesia. At the Japan-China-Korea summit meeting on October 7, Prime Minister Junichiro Koizumi, Prime Minister Wen Jiabao, and

President Roh Moo-hyun signed The Joint Declaration on the Promotion of Tripartite Cooperation, the first trilateral joint documents by the leaders of Japan, China, and South Korea. With the joint declaration, the heads of Government/State of Japan, China and Korea confirmed to promote and strengthen the trilateral cooperation in the new century from a future-oriented perspective.[39]

On the same day, at the first meeting between Prime Minister Koizumi and Prime Minister Wen Jiabao, Premier Wen requested that the poisonous gas accident in Qiqihar be dealt with promptly and appropriately, and that this be an opportunity to accelerate the destruction of abandoned chemical weapons in China.[40]

(2) Official-level consultation and final settlement

The Japan-China official-level consultation on the Qiqihar poisonous gas accident took place three times in Beijing, from September 3 to 4, September 9, and October 13 to 15, between officials from the Ministry of Foreign Affairs and the Cabinet Office of Japan and officials from the Ministry of Foreign Affairs of China. The two sides confirmed the final settlement between Japan and China in a document between the two governments on October 19, and the content was announced on the same day. In this paper, I would like to introduce the issues discussed in the official-level consultation in line with the contents confirmed in the document, and for reference, I would like to post the announcement made on the same day as document material at the end.

The Japanese government's concern in the official-level consultation was how to settle the poisonous gas accident in general, but more specifically how to deal with the poisonous gas accident caused by the chemical weapons of the former Japanese army in the situation where there had not existed war related claim issues after the issuance of Japan-China Joint Communique in 1972. Naturally, the Japanese government could not take measures that could be understood as compensation for individual victims. On the other hand, it was necessary to minimize the impact of this accident on the execution of the destruction project of abandoned chemical weapons and, eventually on Japan-China relations in general. Finding a way to meet these two demands at the same time and reach an agreement with the Chinese side was the challenge for the Japanese officials involved in the consultation.

The basic idea of the Japanese government was, while upholding the Japan-China Joint Communique of 1972, to show a sincere response to this poisonous gas accident through applying the framework and approach of the destruction project of abandoned chemical weapons in China, which had been promoted by Japan under the Chemical Weapons Convention. In the implementation of the field survey that started in 1995, and the large-scale excavation and recovery operation that started in 2000, Japan had sought the cooperation of Chinese authorities in many fields such as installation of a protective dome and manual labor for excavation, etc. Under the Chemical Weapons Convention, Japan is obliged to provide all necessary funds, technology, experts, facilities and other resources for the destruction of abandoned chemical weapons. Therefore, Japan had implemented each operation by burdening the expense for such cooperation.

Even in response to the poisonous gas accident in Qiqihar City, if the drum-shaped container that caused the accident had been found intact, it would surely have been assessed and sealed with the cooperation of the Chinese side under the framework of the field survey. In such a case, Japan would also have borne the costs incurred on the Chinese side. On the other hand, in the usual field survey, the work had been carried out after taking all possible safety measures such as blocking the excavation site and evacuating the local residents. In Qiqihar's case, the damage had expanded due to the fact that the drum-shaped container had been transported multiple times and the contaminated construction surplus soil had also been transported to multiple points. Therefore, it was necessary for the official-level consultation to decide how to grasp the cost incurred by the Chinese authorities in dealing with such a sudden and unexpected accident.

The document between the two Governments dated October 19, 2003, showed a consensus between the Japanese and Chinese Governments on such issues.

First, the document specifically mentions the Japan-China Joint Communique, the Chemical Weapons Convention, and the Japan-China Memorandum of Understanding in 1999 at its beginning. These references are meant to reconfirm the position that there had been no claim issue related to the previous war between the two countries. Based upon such reconfirmation, it showed measures would be taken as part of Japan's abandoned chemical weapons destruction project under the Chemical Weapons Convention, which was created after the issuance of the Japan-China Joint Communique and to which both countries became parties.

The second and third paragraphs described the occurrence of the poisonous gas accident and the subsequent response of both the Japanese and Chinese governments. Then, in the fourth paragraph, the Government of Japan announced that it would tender 300 million yen for the abandoned chemical weapons destruction project, and the two Governments confirmed that the remedial issues related to the accident would be finally settled with the tender by Japan. In addition, the outbreak of the poisonous gas accident in Qiqihar reaffirmed the importance of establishing a thorough medical system in advancing the abandoned chemical weapons destruction project. Therefore, in the fifth paragraph, the two Governments confirmed that a specific study would be conducted to investigate and establish the medical system at the site.

(3) Japan-China Summit Meeting (October 20, Bangkok)

The 2003 Asia-Pacific Economic Cooperation (APEC) Summit was held in Bangkok, Thailand on October 20 and 21, and Prime Minister Koizumi had his second Japan-China summit with President Hu Jintao on October 20. At this meeting, Prime Minister Koizumi pointed out that the two governments had reached an agreement on the Qiqihar poisonous gas accident, and made it clear that Japan would continue to deal with the issue of abandoned chemical weapons in good faith. Whereas, President Hu replied that the issue of chemical weapons had been a problem left by history and was a real problem, and that the remedial issue related to this accident had been agreed through the official-level consultation, and requested Japan to accelerate the destruction of chemical weapons. It was the moment that the final settlement agreed upon in Beijing one day before the meeting was confirmed at the summit level of the two countries.[41]

Epilogue

This paper was written for Professor Ando Nisuke's, Jubilee Publishing. When I was invited to write a paper for Professor Ando's Jubilee book, what came to my mind was the garden of Tenryuji Temple in Kyoto in February 1987, almost 20 years ago. At that time, I was an official of the China Division of the Asian Bureau of the Ministry of Foreign Affairs of Japan, and guided a group of Chinese international law experts to visit Dr. Ashibe Nobuyoshi, Dr. Higuchi Yoichi, Dr. Hatano Satoshi, and Dr. Sawaki Takao in Tokyo. We exchanged opinions on Japan's separation of powers, international law, and private international law. In Kyoto, we visited Professors Tabata Shigejiro and Ando Nisuke and had a discussion at the Kyodai Kaikan (Kyoto University Hall). This Chinese delegation of international law experts was attended by Professor Wang Houli, who would later become the chairman of the China International Law Association, and Professor Ma Jun, who later became the vice chairman and secretary-general of the Association. At the meetings, there were sometimes sharp conflicts and exchanges; however, at the end of the series of schedules, Professor Ando took everybody to have lunch at Seizan Sodo in Kyoto Tenryuji Temple. We all looked at the garden in the soft winter sun while poking hot tofu, and talked about the diligence of Chinese students studying at Kyoto University graduate school and the Japan-China exchange in the field of international law. Professor Ando told us that although there were various disagreements and conflicts between Japan and China, it was important to deepen understanding step by step through exchanges and discussions.

If Japan and China deal with the problem of abandoned chemical weapons on the common basis of the Chemical Weapons Convention, it has the potential to sublimate the problems left by the previous war into a future-oriented cooperative relationship. We hope that the remedial issue related to the Qiqihar poisonous gas accident discussed in this paper will be a step toward building such a cooperative relationship. Finally, I would like to thank Mr. Kawakami, assistant director of the China Division, who led the team of experts to the site on the day after the accident notification, completed the investigation and visited the hospital under the strict eyes of the local residents and the Chinese press. I would also like to thank Mr. Okawa, official of the China Division seconded from the National Police Agency, who directed the sealing and packing operation of the container at the site and exchanged a confirmation letter with the Chinese side. My gratitude also goes to Mr. Fujii, Counselor of the Cabinet Office, Mr. Hamamoto, assistant director of the International Law Division, and Mr. Arima, assistant director of the China Division, who had attended the three rounds of Japan-China official-level consultation together. My profound thanks also goes to Dr. Asari, Dr. Yamaguchi and Dr. Arai, who gave up their summer holidays and participated with the medical expert team in Qiqihar.

Appendix

(Document Material)
Full text of the public announcement made by the Embassy of Japan in China on October 19, 2003

As a result of consultation between Japan and China, the final settlement to the poisonous gas accident in Qiqihar City, Heilongjiang Province, China was confirmed in writing on October 19, and the outline is as follows.

1. Based on the Japan-China Joint Communique, the Chemical Weapons Convention and the Japan-China Memorandum of Understanding in 1999, the Japanese and Chinese governments discussed to settle the issue of the poisonous gas accident in Qiqihar City on August 4, this year (hereinafter referred to as the "accident").

2. The Chinese government has stated that the accident caused great damage, one person died and 43 people were injured, and that the Chinese side timely treated the contaminated site and medically treated the injured. The Chinese side also stated that the Japanese

Government must take it seriously, handle it appropriately, and settle it promptly.

3. From the standpoint of sincerely responding to the accident, the Government of Japan dispatched a team to confirm the facts and conducted an on-site investigation. The team confirmed that the five drums that had caused the accident were abandoned chemical weapons of Japan. The Japanese Government also dispatched a team of experts to seal and pack the drums, and medical experts to exchange opinions with Chinese medical personnel. The Government of Japan reiterated that it would take appropriate measures regarding the destruction of abandoned chemical weapons, including accelerating the destruction project, with the cooperation of the Chinese side, in accordance with the Chemical Weapons Convention and the Japan-China Memorandum of Understanding.

4. In connection with the accident, the Government of Japan stated that it would tender 300 million yen for the abandoned chemical weapons destruction operation, and the Chinese government stated that it would take responsibility to distribute this fund appropriately to the related parties. With this, the Japanese and Chinese governments confirmed the final settlement to the remedial issue related to the accident.

5. Both sides believe that it is necessary to study and establish a medical system that is indispensable for accident response in the abandoned chemical weapons destruction project based on the Chemical Weapons Convention and the Japan-China Memorandum of Understanding. It was confirmed that specific consideration would be given to this point during the discussions between Japan and China.

Notes

1   "Chief Cabinet Secretary Fukuda visits China", *Asahi Shimbun*, August 10, 2003. "Chinese Prime Minister considers Yasukuni Shrine visits as a problem, to Secretary Fukuda", *Asahi Shimbun*, August 11, 2003, evening edition.

2   "Japan-China Summit Meeting at APEC Summit (Summary)" (www. mofa.go.jp, October 20, 2003).

3   "Abandoned Chemical Weapon of the Former Japanese Army; All
    Records of Qiqihar Injury Case", *Heilongjiang Daily*, August 10, 2003
    (Nanfang Net, China News www.southcn.com).

4   "The Former Japanese Army's toxic agent in China caused injury,
    Foreign Ministry Protest against Japanese Side", *Xinhua News Agency*,
    August 9, 2003.

5   Cabinet Office Abandoned Chemical Weapons Destruction Office,
    "Overview of the Former Japanese Army Abandoned Chemical
    Weapons Destruction Project in China" (www8.cao.go.jp, October,
    2002).

6   Cabinet Office Abandoned Chemical Weapons Destruction Office,
    "About issue of the Abandoned Chemical Weapons in China" (www8.
    cao.go.jp, July 2004).

7   Akio Suda, General Manager, Abandoned Chemical Weapons De-
    struction Office, Prime Minister's Office "Working on the Abandoned
    Chemical Weapons Destruction Project", *Diplomatic Forum*, September
    2000 issue.

8   Although the Geneva Protocol of 1925 prohibited "the use in war of
    asphyxiating, poisonous or other gases", it did not prohibit its develop-
    ment, production and storage. "Outline of the Chemical Weapons
    Convention (CWC)" (www.mofa.go.jp, March 2005).

9   Tadashi Ikeda's Parliamentary statement, "Minutes of the Budget Com-
    mittee of the House of Representatives 126th session" No. 14 (February
    25, 1993), pp. 30-31, Foreign Minister Yohei Kono's Parliamentary
    statement, "Minutes of the Foreign Affairs Committee of the House of
    Councilors 132nd session" No. 10 (April 25, 1995), p. 7.

10 Foreign Minister Michio Watanabe's Speech on Diplomacy, "Minutes
    of the House of Representatives 123rd session" No. 1 (1) (January 24,
    1992), p. 6.

11 Tadashi Ikeda's Parliamentary statement, "Minutes of the Foreign Af-
    fairs Committee of the House of Representatives 126th session" No. 14
    (June 11, 1993), p. 19.

12 "Outline of the Chemical Weapons Convention (CWC)" (www.mofa.
    go.jp, March 2005).

13 Yutaka Kawashima's Parliamentary statement, "Minutes of the Foreign
    Affairs Committee of the House of Councilors 132nd session" No. 3
    (February 28, 1995), p. 5.

14 "Unexploded ordnance removed in Nishitokyo City, 7,000 residents
    temporarily evacuated", *Kyodo News*, July 10, 2005.

15 "Convention on the Prohibition of the Development, Production,
    Stockpiling and Use of Chemical Weapons and on their Destruction,
    Annex on Implementation and Verification", Part IV (B) 15.

16 Cabinet Office Abandoned Chemical Weapons Destruction Office, "Overview of the former Japanese Army Abandoned Chemical Weapons Destruction Project in China" (www8.cao.go.jp, October, 2002).

17 Foreign Minister Yohei Kono's Parliamentary statement, "Minutes of the Foreign Affairs Committee of the House of Councilors 132nd session" No. 10 (April 25, 1995), p. 7.

18 Ryozo Kato's Parliamentary statement, "The Minutes of the Budget Committee of the House of Representatives 136th session" No. 24 (April 3, 1996), p. 2.

19 "Convention on the Prohibition of the Development, Production, Stockpiling and Use of Chemical Weapons and on their Destruction" promulgated on April 21, 1997.

20 "Japanese Foreign Ministry official arrived at the August 4 poisonous gas leak sites", *Xinhua News Agency*, From Harbin, August 10, 2003.

21 "Expert Appraises Poisonous Gas as Mustard Gas, Four Representatives of Japan arrive in Qiqihar", *Heilongjiang Daily*, August 10, 2003 (From Yunnan Xinxi Port www.yninfo.com).

22 "Foreign Minister Li Zhaoxing Meets Japanese Prime Minister Junichiro Koizumi", *Xinhua News Agency*, From Tokyo, August 11, 2003.

23 "Statement by the Press Secretary/Director-General for Press and Public Relations, Ministry of Foreign Affairs, on the poison gas accident in Qiqihar City, Heilongjiang Province" (www.mofa.go.jp, August 12, 2003).

24 "Wang Yi Meets Ambassador to China, Lodges Solemn Representations again on Poisonous Injury Case", *China News Service*, From Beijing, August 12, 2003.

25 *People's Daily*, August 13, 2003.

26 *Global Times*, August 13, 2003.

27 "Press Release: Dispatch of a team of medical experts for poisonous gas accidents in the northeastern region of China (Qiqihar City, Heilongjiang Province)" (www.mofa.go.jp, August 14, 2003, four days).

28 "Japanese Medical Experts Group arrives in Qiqihar, to Experiment the Destruction of Abandoned Chemical Weapon ", *China News Service*, From Qiqihar, August 16, 2003.

29 Kanagawa Prefecture Safety and Disaster Prevention Bureau, "On Response to the dangerous material found at the Sagami Transit Road Construction Site, Former Sagami Navy Factory Site in Samukawa Town" (www.pref.kanagawa.jp, December, 2004), "Current Situation of the Aging Chemical Weapons Destruction Problem of the Former Japanese Army in Japan" (www.mofa.go.jp, April 2004).

30 *People's Daily, Beijing Youth Daily, Heilongjiang Daily, Jilin Daily*, all on August 17, 2003.

31 "Statement by the Press Secretary/Director-General for Press and Public Relations, Ministry of Foreign Affairs, on the Poison Gas Accident in Qiqihar City, Heilongjiang Province" (www.mofa.go.jp, August 22, 2003).

32 Cabinet Office Abandoned Chemical Weapons Destruction Office, "About issue of the Abandoned Chemical Weapons in China" (www8. cao.go.jp, July 2004).

33 "Memorandum of Understanding between Japan and China on the Destruction of Abandoned Chemical Weapons in China" (www8.cao. go.jp, July 30, 1999).

34 Akio Suda, General Manager, Abandoned Chemical Weapons Destruction Office, Prime Minister's Office "Working on 'Abandoned Chemical Weapons Destruction Project'", *Diplomatic Forum*, September 2000 issue. "Former Japanese Army Abandoned Chemical Weapons in China, Destruction Project Overview (www8.cao.go.jp, October 2002).

35 "Implementation of abandoned chemical weapons excavation and recovery operation in China (Ning'an, Heilongjiang Province)" (www8.cao.go.jp, August 26, 2004). "Completion of abandoned chemical weapons excavation and recovery operation in Ning'an, Heilongjiang Province, China" (www8.cao.go.jp, September 27, 2004).

36 "Recent Development of the issue of Abandoned Chemical Weapons in China" (www8.cao.go.jp, April 22, 2004).

37 "Wu Bangguo Meets Junichiro Koizumi, Japan's Prime Minister Expresses Condolences to the Victim of the Japanese Poisonous Agent", *China News Service*, September 5, 2003.

38 "Ms. Yoriko Kawaguchi, Minister for Foreign Affairs, Attends the 58th UN General Assembly (Summary)" (www.mofa.go.jp, September 26, 2003). "Japan-China Foreign Ministers' Meeting at the UN General Assembly (Summary)" (www.mofa.go.jp, September 24, 2003).

39 "Joint Declaration on the Promotion of Tripartite Cooperation among Japan, the People's Republic of China and the Republic of Korea" (www.mofa.go.jp, October 7, 2003).

40 "Japan-China Summit Meeting at the ASEAN + 3 Summit Meeting" (www.mofa.go.jp, October 7, 2003).

41 "Japan-China Summit Meeting at APEC Summit (Summary)" (www.mofa.go.jp, October 20, 2003).

Chapter IV

Waters

Spy Vessel Incident in the Southwest Waters of Kyushu

Introduction

On March 6, 2002, at a press conference at the National People's Congress in China, Foreign Minister Tang Jiaxuan raised his voice in response to a reporter's question. "The Chinese side ... expresses strong dissatisfaction with the Japanese side's careless use of force in the exclusive economic zone of the Chinese side and the sinking of the vessel ... We insist that Japan respects the rights and concerns of the Chinese side on this case, and will not take actions that may make the situation worse and more complicated".[1] This was the moment when it was revealed to the outside that China did not want "salvage", which could lead to "a worse and more complicated situation". However, in October of the same year, seven months after this statement, the "China Marine Bulletin" posted a commentary that highly evaluated the salvage. It reported that the salvage of the suspicious ship "had established an example for reasonably settling the dispute and dealing with a case that could occur in the exclusive economic zones".[2] During these seven months, the Japanese side, in order to elucidate the whole picture of the suspicious ship incident,[3] conducted a manned diving survey from May 1 to 8 and carried out the hull's salvage successfully from June 25 to September 14 with the cooperation of the Chinese side. Throughout 2002, this North Korean spy vessel incident was widely reported, with details on the large amount of weapons found, special hull structures, and various evidence including mobile phones. However, the successive talks between Japan and China, that had been held to gain the understanding and cooperation of the Chinese side regarding the salvage had not been widely reported. In this paper, I would like to look back on the handling of the suspicious ship incident, which was highly evaluated by the Chinese side, by giving an overview of the issues under international law discussed at the Japan-China talks.

The author was directly involved in the handling of the incident and the negotiations with China as the director of the Legal Affairs Division of the Treaty Bureau at the time of the suspicious ship incident, and as the director of the China Division, Asian and Oceanian Affairs Bureau of the Ministry of Foreign Affairs of Japan after April 2002. However, this article is the sole responsibility of the author, and the views expressed in this article do not represent the views of the Government or the Ministry of Foreign Affairs of Japan, except for the direct citations such as the parliamentary statement and the external announcement, etc.

First appearance of the paper: "Suspicious Ship Incident in the Southwest Waters of Kyushu and International Law", *Waseda Law Review*, September 2003, Vol. 79-1.

1. Outbreak of incident

(1) Outline of the incident

Before dawn on December 22, 2001, the Japan Coast Guard received information provided by the Defense Agency and started tracking a suspicious foreign fishing vessel in the northwestern waters of Amami Oshima. Upon arriving at the site, Coast Guard Patrol Vessel Inasa requested the suspicious ship to stop for on-site inspection under the Fisheries Act. However, the ship ignored the stop order and continued to sail, so at 14:36, the Patrol Vessel warned and threatened to fire. However, even with these warnings and the threat of shooting, the suspicious ship did not stop and passed through the Japan-China median line. After 16:00, Patrol Vessels Inasa and Mizuki fired on the hull for intimidation. At 22:09, two Patrol Vessels tried to sandwich the suspicious ship to prevent it from further escaping, but the Patrol Vessels received attacks by something like an automatic rifle and a rocket launcher. The Patrol Vessels Amami, Kirishima, and Inasa were hit, and three coast guard officers were injured. When the Patrol Vessel Inasa fired in self-defense against these attacks, the suspicious ship exploded and sank.[4]

(2) Examination at the stage of incident occurrence

At the stage when the above incident occurred, the Government departments of Japan continued various communications and examinations.

First, is it possible to carry out threatening shooting against suspicious foreign fishing vessels that ignore the stop order and escape within Japan's exclusive economic zone? In this regard, based on the provisions of Article 73-1 of the United Nations Convention on the Law of the Sea (hereinafter referred to as the UNCLOS), it was confirmed that the coastal state might, in the exercise of its sovereign rights to explore, exploit, conserve and manage the living resources in the exclusive economic zone, take necessary measures to ensure compliance with relevant laws and regulations. These necessary measures include stopping fishing boats, etc. that operate without permission. The Japanese government judged that if it is unavoidable to implement these orders, the use of weapons was permitted to a reasonable limit when it is premised that the necessary conditions such as giving a warning by a signal etc. are satisfied.[5]

Second, is it possible to "pursue" a vessel that ignores the stop order and continues to flee beyond the limits of the exclusive economic zone? According to Article 1 of the Act on the Exclusive Economic Zone and the Continental Shelf of Japan, Japan's exclusive economic zone in the East China Sea is understood as the water area up to the Japan-China median line. Therefore, in order to "pursue" this suspicious foreign fishing vessel beyond the Japan-China median line, a basis under international law was required. The exercise of the right of hot pursuit from the exclusive economic zone is stipulated in Article 111-2 of the UNCLOS. When the Coastal State has good reason to believe that the foreign ship has violated the relevant laws and regulations of the State in its exclusive economic zone, the State may pursue the foreign ship until it enters the territorial sea of its own state or of a third state. Therefore, it was possible to "pursue" a vessel that violated the Fisheries Act within the exclusive economic zone of Japan and escaped. In addition, the Government of Japan judged that, along with this hot pursuit, the use of weapons to the necessary and reasonable limits was permitted on the premise that the necessary conditions such as giving a warning by a signal were met.[6]

(3) Examination of the sinking of the suspicious ship

However, the examination on December 22 did not end at the applicability test of "the right of hot pursuit". The development of the situation, sinking of the suspicious ship at midnight, forced further consideration. With respect to the sinking, it became clear later by the salvage investigation that it had been caused by self-destructive actions using some explosives.[7] However, the cause of the sinking was unknown at the stage of the outbreak of the incident and the Japanese Government could not rule out the possibility that it had been the result of shooting out of self-defense by the Patrol Vessels. In this regard, a comparative study was conducted with international precedents regarding cases of vessel pursuit. The reports of international arbitration were referred, like the cases of Canadian vessel I'm Alone (1929), which was pursued and shot by the US Coast Guard on suspicion of smuggling alcohol and sank,[8] and the British vessel Red Crusader (1962), which was damaged by the shooting of a Danish guard vessel during pursuit.[9] In addition, the Marianna Flora case (1826), which showed judgment on access rights and inspections of unidentified vessels on the high seas, and the M/V Saiga case (1999), in which a decision on the use of weapons was shown,[10] were examined. After the examination, the Government of Japan reconfirmed that in case of hot pursuit of a fleeing vessel that was ignoring repeated stop orders, the international law did not prohibit the use of weapons to a reasonable limit under the necessary conditions such as giving a warning by a signal etc.[11]

(4) Concerns of the Chinese side and response of Japan

After the outbreak of the suspicious vessel incident, a Chinese Foreign Ministry spokesman confirmed in Beijing that the sunken vessel was not a Chinese vessel, while saying, "Japan used force in the process of pursuing a vessel of unknown nationality and China expresses serious concern over the sinking of the vessel in China's economic waters".[12] In order to respond to such concerns on the Chinese side, Japan explained the overall situation of the case at the beginning of the Japan-China Law of the Sea Consultation held in Tokyo on December 25. The Japanese side's explanation had two major points. The first point was that the actions of the Japan Coast Guard Patrol Vessels had been legal in accordance with the United Nations Convention on the Law of the Sea in all aspects like stop order, warning, threatening shooting, and pursuit. The second point was that the Japan Coast Guard's actions on that day had been part of the police action allowed to crack down on violations of the laws and regulations applicable in the exclusive economic zone. Therefore, the shooting by Japanese law enforcement vessels did not fall under the "use of force" prohibited by Article 2 of the Charter of the United Nations, and there was no need for concern on the Chinese side.

The Japanese side repeated this explanation whenever China expressed their concerns, but the statement by the Chinese Foreign Minister on March 6 (see *Introduction*) showed that not all Chinese officials had known about the explanation. Immediately after this statement, however, Japanese Vice-Minister for Foreign Affairs Yukio Takeuchi argued that the actions of the Japan Coast Guard Patrol Vessel were "a natural response as a sovereign state and a law-abiding country, and were by no means careless." His argument was reported afterwards,[13] and after the report, the Chinese side did not repeat the criticism of "improper use of force" in public.

2. Toward the Salvage

(1) Challenges faced

Following the suspicious vessel incident, the challenge the Japanese government faced in the investigation to clarify the facts was the co-ordination with China. The site where the suspicious vessel sank is a sea area that Japan, in effect, treats as China's exclusive econom-ic zone; under the United Nations Convention on the Law of the Sea, coastal states have jurisdiction over the marine environment and sovereign rights over natural resources. Immediately after the outbreak of the incident, the Japan Coast Guard patrol vessels pre-served the hull and other evidence of the sunken suspicious vessel at the site of this sea area, with the result that Chinese fishermen who were unable to operate freely expressed strong dissatisfaction with the Chinese government. If the hull was to be withdrawn, a series of procedures would be required. First, a survey to identify the sinking position, then a manned diving survey with the aim of obtaining the information necessary to determine the possibility of the withdrawal. If judged that it was technically possible, it would be necessary to start the actual salvage work while observing the weather condi-tions.[14] In other words, it was expected that the impact on fishery production would expand due to the prolongation of the vigilance period at the site, while the possibility of marine pollution caused by oil leaks due to the salvage work was not ruled out. So it became necessary to make appropriate adjustments to the sovereign rights and jurisdiction of the coastal state.

Under the United Nations Convention on the Law of the Sea, each state shall have due regard to the rights and duties of coastal states and shall comply with the laws and regulations adopted by the coastal state when exercising their rights in the exclusive economic zone of other states (Article 56, 58-3). Therefore, in order to coordin-ate with the Chinese side, it was a necessary task in advance to clarify that it was Japan's right to withdraw this suspicious vessel. In other words, Japan had to find the grounds under international law that made it possible to claim that it was the right of its own to salvage a sunken vessel that had a risk of marine pollution, etc. in the sea area in effect treated as the exclusive economic zone of another state. Finding such grounds became the biggest challenge facing Japan.

(2) International law on salvage

The task of finding the rules on salvage under international law turned out to be extremely difficult. The salvage of sunken ships is usually carried out by private businesses for the purpose of processing stranded vessels or withdrawing treasure. There have been few cases in which a state has withdrawn vessels. It meant that there had not been enough practice at national level in the world. Past cases examined by the Japanese government showed nothing more than the fact that those precedents have consistently taken the position that, when withdrawing warships or other public vessels, consent of the home government was required.[15]

On the other hand, what had become clear through such examinations was that there were no rules under international law that regulated the withdrawal of a private vessel when it had sunken in the high seas.[16] Therefore, in such a case, if Japan withdrew a sunken vessel of unknown owner as part of a criminal investigation, it would not cause any problems under international law. If we dared to seek the grounds for this, it was understood that it would result in "freedom of the high seas."

(3) Political work

While the government department continued to consider issues under international law, political efforts were made from a high level with China.

In April 2002, Foreign Minister Kawaguchi introduced to Mr. Li Peng, the Chairman of the National People's Congress of China, who visited Japan to celebrate the 30th anniversary of the normalization of diplomatic relations, that there were many voices in Japan insisting on the withdrawal of the suspicious vessel and asked for the understanding of the Chinese side. In response, Chairman Li Peng said, "I understand the high interest of the Japanese people in the suspicious vessel issue. In light of international and domestic law, we should find a method that is acceptable to both sides. I have a positive attitude towards this matter." During his visit to Japan, he also told Prime Minister Koizumi that the two sides should find a solution that would satisfy both Japan and China by having the relevant departments discuss the issue of the suspicious vessel.

Furthermore, in the same month, Prime Minister Koizumi, who visited Hainan Island in China and attended the first Boao Forum for Asia, held a meeting with Premier Zhu Rongji and raised the issue of the suspicious vessel at the summit level. At this meeting, Premire Zhu Rongji said, "The Chinese government intends to resolve the issue of the suspicious vessel through discussions with the Japanese side based on international and domestic law. The diplomatic authorities have already begun discussions. The talks should proceed calmly. I believe that this problem can be solved without fail." Intergovernmental talks to achieve this summit-level agreement to "seek a mutually satisfying solution through calm discussions" would continue afterwards.

3. Conclusion of Japan-China talks

Japan-China talks on the salvage of the suspicious vessel had been held intermittently from mid-April 2002, despite the occurrence of the Prime Minister's visit to Yasukuni Shrine and the case of the Consulate General of Shenyang. Six meetings were held in total up to the conclusion on June 18. This series of discussions can be divided into two parts, which were two meetings for the realization of a manned diving survey and four meetings for the salvage of the hull itself based on the results of such survey. Both the discussion on a manned diving survey and on the salvage of the hull had issues in common. In this paper, I would like to introduce the outline of the discussion in line with the contents confirmed by issuing *notes verbale* between Japan and China on June 18. The public announcement made at the conclusion of the Japan-China talks clarified the contents of the *notes verbale* and I post it at the end of this paper for reference.

(1) Grounds for criminal investigation and salvage

The attitude of the Chinese side at the first meeting in April was extremely strict. They again expressed strong suspicions on the actions of the Japan Coast Guard patrol vessels at the end of December of the previous year. They also raised issues caused by the deployment of multiple Japanese patrol vessels on-site after the incident, such as the inability of Chinese fishermen to operate at their traditional fishing grounds and the hindrance of the activities of Chinese law-enforcement vessels. The Chinese side expressed strong dissatisfaction at this situation and asked the Japanese side to clarify the grounds in international law to continue such a situation for a long period and even to conduct submersible surveys and salvage.

The Japanese side explained that the activities of the patrol vessels in December of the previous year were legal in accordance with international and domestic laws and the deployment of the multiple Japanese patrol vessels on site since the incident was the measure to maintain the current situation of the sunk suspicious vessel and to preserve evidence. The Japanese side further argued that if the case had happened on the high seas, Japan would have been able to carry out the diving investigation and salvage as part of the criminal investigation without any problems and that coastal states, when exercising their rights in the exclusive economic zone, should give due consideration to the rights of other countries under the "freedom of the high seas".[17]

The issue of what is the basis of international law for the on-site deployment of Japanese patrol vessels, submersible surveys, and salvage of the hull was repeatedly discussed through successive consultations. Finally, the two sides reached agreement to refer to the provisions of the United Nations Convention on the Law of the Sea on marine utilization at the beginning of the *notes verbale*. Those provisions were Article 56-2 and 58-3, that said marine using states should give due consideration to the rights of coastal states when exercising their rights, and coastal states should also give due consideration to the rights of maritime users when exercising their rights. In other words, after recognizing the diving survey and salvage as

Japan's rights, it was decided to reach a conclusion by confirming that both Japan and China would give due consideration to each other's rights.

(2) Application of domestic law

The next issue was the application of Chinese domestic law. The party actually in charge of the diving survey and salvage was a Japanese private company commissioned by the Japan Coast Guard, and the Chinese government could have requested an application for work from the company in accordance with Chinese domestic laws concerning marine pollution, etc., and could have given permission based on such laws. On the other hand, the Japanese side was in the position that the investigation and salvage were to be carried out as part of the criminal investigation regarding violations of laws and regulations of Japan, and it was unacceptable that such investigation would take the form of obtaining "permits" from other countries. However, it was natural for Japan to "comply with the laws and regulations adopted by coastal countries in accordance with the provisions of this Convention and other rules of international law," stipulated by the UN-CLOS. Japan also had no objection to confirming the provisions of the Convention that Japan would give due consideration to the rights and obligations of coastal states (Article 58-3).

The conclusion of the Japan-China talks, obtained after the exchange of the above-mentioned fundamental positions of both sides, was as follows: China would not request an "application" from a company of Japan in accordance with its domestic laws and regulations. On the other hand, the Japanese side would provide the information through diplomatic channels such as a detailed work plan and alert system, etc., which would be necessary for the Chinese side to proceed with the examination. The Chinese side would proceed with the examination after receiving such information, and would not object to the investigation and salvage by the Japanese side.

(3) On-site Japan-China cooperation

As important as achieving a common understanding between the two governments was securing cooperation between Japanese and

Chinese public vessels in the working sea area. The Chinese public vessels were dissatisfied with the fact that several Japan Coast Guard patrol vessels had been deployed continuously on-site since immediately after the incident, hindering the Chinese side's law enforcement activities. Therefore, there was an urgent need to build a cooperative relationship between them based on mutual trust. The *notes verbale* exchanged between Japan and China on June 18 described this point in detail, including coordination on the start and end times of work, the number of work vessels, and the number of alert vessels and aircrafts. They also confirmed that there was a consensus between Japan and China regarding cooperation with Chinese law enforcement vessels and the establishment of a contact point in the sea area at the site.

In addition, how to proceed with the request for cooperation from Chinese fishing vessels, which had used the field sea area as their traditional fishing areas, was also an issue at the meeting. In conducting the manned diving survey and salvage, it was necessary to lower the atmospheric divers to the seabed about 100 meters below the surface of the water. However, if by any chance a fishing boat or fishing net should cut the cable connecting the divers with the mother ship, this would immediately cause a life-threatening situation. Both Japan and China agreed that it was necessary to prevent Chinese fishing vessels from approaching the sea area in order to ensure smooth and safe work, but there was a strong reservation on the part of the Chinese side that too many Japanese vessels were to be deployed on-site. As a result of the discussion, the Chinese side would be responsible for all restrictions on the access of Chinese fishing vessels, and the Japanese side would cooperate with their access control. The statement "the Japanese side will cooperate in supervision and management (by Chinese law enforcement vessels)" stated in the *notes verbale* reflected these arguments.[18]

(4) Dealing with environmental problems

The danger of marine pollution is always a problem when a sunken ship is withdrawn, and at the salvage of the suspicious vessel it was decided to take all necessary measures including preventing oil spills by sealing the places where there was a risk of oil leakage in the water.

In addition, when withdrawing, measures were to be taken to minimize the roll-up of mud and sand on the seabed so as not to cause an impact on the environment. However, no matter how thorough the environmental measures were to be taken, the possibility of pollution was not completely eliminated, so the Chinese side was in a position to specify in the *notes verbale* that, if such a situation occured, the Japanese side would provide compensation. Regarding this point as well, discussions were repeated between the Japanese side, which insisted on environmental safety, and the Chinese side, which insisted on the need for specifying compensation in the unlikely event of an accident. Finally, both sides reached an agreement to include the following language in the *notes verbale*, that is "if pollution occurs, the Japanese side will respond in accordance with international law."

(5) Dissatisfaction of Chinese fishermen

The biggest issue left for the salvage of the suspicious vessel was how to deal with the dissatisfaction of Chinese fishermen who had been unable to operate in the sea area for a long time. "How do you explain to local fishermen that the Japanese patrol vessels do not show any signs of leaving even half a year after the incident, and that they will further expand the alert sea area and start full-scale salvage?" The remarks made by Chinese fishery authority officials at the Japan-China talks were urgent. The Japanese side also highly valued the fact that Chinese fishermen refrained from operating around the site sea area by taking evasive action in cooperation with the Japanese criminal investigation. However, in the process of discussions to mid-June, it was practically impossible to reach a conclusion on this issue. Therefore, regarding the impact on the operations of Chinese fishermen, the two governments managed to reach a conclusion in the form of continuous talks, by stating in the Japanese *note verbale* that "the Japanese side will continue to seriously consider the demands of the Chinese side and respond in good faith as soon as possible."

Discussions between Japan and China on this fishery issue started in July after the start of the salvage work. There was a large gap between the two Governments regarding the evaluation of the impact of a series of activities by the Japanese side on the operations of Chinese fishermen. Therefore, the discussion continued for several rounds, and finally on December 28, 2002, three months after the end of the salvage and one year after the incident, the two sides reached an agreement. On that day, the two Governments confirmed their settlement by a document ("Record of Discussion") that the Government of China would receive from Japan a total of 150 million yen on behalf of all related Chinese fishermen as an investigation cooperation fund.[19]

Epilogue

The conclusion of the Japan-China talks was confirmed between Foreign Minister Yoriko Kawaguchi and Foreign Minister Tang Jiaxuan at the Japan-China Foreign Ministers' Meeting held in Thailand on June 19, the day after the exchange of *notes verbale*. The Government of Japan, following the conclusion of the talks, officially decided to undertake the salvage of the suspicious vessel at the cabinet meeting on June 21. The actual salvage work had been prolonged due to the effects of typhoons that occurred continuously in July. The hull was recovered on September 11, and all the work vessels left the site on September 14. Many reports have been made that, by the salvage of the hull, the actual condition of the spy vessel which had a unique structure was obtained, and a large amount of important criminal evidence such as weapons and electronic devices was secured.[20]

If, in the future, a law-enforcement vessel from another country enters Japan's exclusive economic zone in the form of a hot pursuit of a suspicious vessel and the suspicious vessel sinks in that water area, how will the Japanese public react? In addition, what will be the tone of the Japanese people in a situation where multiple patrol vessels of another country are deployed in the waters of Japan for a long period trying to undertake salvage despite the dissatisfaction of fishermen? It is hard for me to predict. In that sense, it should be highly evaluated that the Chinese side has consistently adhered to the basic policy of solving the problem through rounds of calm legal discussions. Before concluding this article, I would like to express my deepest gratitude to the people involved in the negotiations on both sides including those from Foreign Ministries, Fishery Agencies and Coast Guards.

Appendix

(Document Material)

Full text of the public announcement made by the Embassy of Japan in China on June 18, 2002.

On June 18, the Japanese side (Embassy in China) issued a *note verbale* to the Chinese side (Foreign Ministry) regarding the issue of the salvage of the suspicious vessel. The Chinese side showed an understanding for the withdrawal work.

The contents of the *note verbale* are as follows.

1. Article 58-3 of the United Nations Convention on the Law of the Sea states that "In exercising their rights and performing their duties under this Convention in the exclusive economic zone, States shall have due regard to the rights and duties of the coastal State and shall comply with the laws and regulations adopted by the coastal State in accordance with the provisions of this Convention and other rules of international law in so far as they are not incompatible with this part. " Article 56-2 of the Convention also states, "In exercising its rights and performing its duties under this Convention in the exclusive economic zone, the coastal State shall have due regard to the rights and duties of other States and shall act in a manner compatible with the provisions of this Convention." Based on this recognition, the Japanese side acknowledges that the Chinese side has sovereign rights and jurisdiction over its exclusive economic zone under the United Nations Convention on the Law of the Sea.

2. Based on the above recognition, the Japanese side hopes that the Chinese side will not object to the salvage of the vessel, in light of the relevant Chinese domestic laws adopted in accordance with the Convention and other rules of international law, after the Japanese side takes the appropriate process.

3. The Japanese side further expresses the following positions regarding the points pointed out by the Chinese side.

    (1) The Japanese side will submit information in advance regarding the start / end time of the withdrawal work and the number of work vessels, and hopes that the Chinese side will respond promptly.

    (2) The number of alert vessels and aircrafts will be finalized through mutual consultation.

    (3) Vessels of Chinese law enforcement agencies will engage in supervision and management in the relevant waters in accordance with the United Nations Convention on the Law of the Sea and related Chinese domestic laws adopted in accordance with the Convention and other rules of international law. The Japanese side will cooperate with such supervision and management.

    (4) The Japanese side will take necessary measures to ensure that the work does not pollute the marine environment during the work period. If pollution occurs, the Japanese side will respond in accordance with international law.

    (5) The Japanese side will notify the Chinese government of the progress of the withdrawal work and its results as before.

    (6) After the work is completed, all vessels on the Japanese side will immediately leave the site and restore the normal condition of the sea area.

    (7) On the matter that the truth-finding investigation by Japan regarding the suspicious vessel case has been affecting the operation of Chinese fishermen in the sea area since the time of the incident to the end of the salvage, the Japanese side will continue to seriously consider the demands of the Chinese side and respond in good faith as soon as possible.

    (8) The Japanese side proposes to establish a contact point between the two governments at the site in the sea area.

Notes

1   "Chinese Foreign Minister Checks Japan on Salvage of Suspicious Ship", *Asahi Shimbun*, March 7, 2002.

2   Lu Rude, "National maritime interests do not allow invasion", *China Maritime Daily*, October 8, 2002.

3   On October 14, 2002, the Japanese government identified the suspicious ship as a North Korean spy vessel (www.kaiho.mlit.go.jp).

4   Japan Coast Guard, "Response to the Suspicious Ship Case in the Southwest Waters of Kyushu" (www.kaiho.mlit.go.jp, December 25, 2001).

5   "Answer to the question regarding the response to the Suspicious Ship Case in the Southwest Waters of Kyushu submitted by Member of the House of Representatives Seiichi Kaneta", Cabinet/ House of Representatives/ Questions No. 154-1 "Government Bulletin (Extra) Minutes of the House of Representatives No. 11 (1)", March 6, 2002, pp. 27-28.

6   "Answer to the question regarding the falsification of facts in the warning shooting in the Suspicious Ship Case in the Southwest Waters of Kyushu submitted by Member of the House of Representatives Seiichi Kaneta", Cabinet/ House of Representatives/ Questions No. 154-156, "Government Bulletin (Extra) Minutes of the House of Representatives Addendum", September 26, 2002, pp. 116-117.

7   Japan Coast Guard, "Investigation status of the spy vessel case in the southwest waters of Kyushu" (www.kaiho.mlit.go.jp, December 6, 2002).

8   Rekizou Murakami, "The right of Hot Pursuit-I'm Alone Case", Jurist Extra Issue, *100 Selections of International Law Cases*, No. 156, Yuhikaku, April 2001, pp. 92-93.

9   Kou Nakamura, "Fact Examination-Red Crusader Case", *100 Selections of International Law Cases*, No. 156, Yuhikaku, April 2001, pp. 158-159.

10 Mamoru Koga, "Commercial Activities in the Exclusive Economic Zone-Saiga (No. 2) Case-", *100 Selections of International Law Cases*, No. 156, Yuhikaku, April 2001, pp. 88-89. Shigeki Sakamoto "The Case of the Suspicious Ship from the Viewpoint of International Law", *World*, No. 699, Iwanami Shoten, March 2002, pp. 20-25.

11 There are also criticisms of pursuing from the exclusive economic zone based on violation of the stop order from the Fisheries Act. Shunji Taoka, "Legal Questions about the Sinking of the Suspicious Ship", *Ships of the World*, Vol. 594, Kaijinsha, April 2002, pp. 148-151.

12 "Respect the Chinese interests in case handling; Chinese Foreign Ministry on the Suspicious Ship Case; China Central Television December 25 = RP", *RP China News Separate Volume*, December 26, 2001, No. 14625.

13 "As a law-abiding country, it is natural to shoot a suspicious ship", *Asahi Shimbun*, March 9, 2002.

14 "Minutes of the 154th Session of the House of Representatives, Security Committee Meeting No. 4" (Category 1, No. 123, April 2, 2002), pp. 12-13.

15 "Minutes of the 93rd Session of the House of Representatives, Settlement Committee Meeting No. 2" (Category 1, No. 16, October 20, 1980), p 10.

16 Soji Yamamoto, "Salvage of Sunken Foreign Ships and Their Ownership," *Law School*, No. 4 (Yuhikaku, January 1981), pp. 61-65. In February 2002, the author met with Soji Yamamoto, a member of the International Tribunal for the Law of the Sea, together with Rumi Ariyoshi, officer of the International Law Division, Treaty Bureau, Ministry of Foreign Affairs (1994, Waseda University Law), and consulted on preparing for the upcoming discussions with China. We explained our argument about the "right" of salvage based on "the freedom of the high-seas" and sought his advice on what to do if the Japanese side's claim of "freedom of the high-seas" and the Chinese side's claim of "coastal sovereign rights and jurisdiction over the exclusive economic zone" were in complete conflict. The professor suggested that it would constitute a "dispute" stipulated in Article 59 of the United Nations Convention on the Law of the Sea as "in case where this Convention does not attribute right or jurisdiction to the coastal State or to other States." The author had intended to raise this suggestion if the Japan-China talks had been a complete stalemate, but the understanding of the Chinese side was obtained without reaching that point as shown in the paper. I would like to take this opportunity to express my deep gratitude to Professor Soji Yamamoto for his advice which supported intergovernmental negotiations.

17 Article 58-1 of the United Nations Convention on the Law of the Sea stipulates that "freedom of the high seas" under Article 87 extends to the exclusive economic zone. The same paragraph also provides that "other internationally lawful use of the sea related to these freedoms, ..., and compatible with the other provisions of this Convention" are also enjoyed in the exclusive economic zone. Therefore, the Japanese side argued that the coastal State has sovereign rights and jurisdiction specified in Article 56 of the UNCLOS; however, except for those fields, "freedom of the high seas" widely extends to the exclusive economic zone.

18 "Diving Survey Area of the Suspicious Ship, closely watched by China Surveillance Vessels", *Yomiuri Shimbun*, May 1, 2002. Some Japanese

newspapers, including this one, reported that "Chinese vessels monitored investigation and withdrawal work," but in reality, Chinese public vessels had been deployed in the sea area to restrict Chinese fishing vessels from access and provide guidance on avoidance actions. Both sides had given high praise for the extremely smooth communication and coordination between the Japanese and Chinese authorities through the series of work.

19 "150 million yen as cooperation money for salvage of the spy ship, agreed between Japan and China", *Mainichi Shimbun*, December 27, 2002.

20 Japan Coast Guard, "Investigation status of the spy ship case in the southwest waters of Kyushu" (www.kaiho.mlit.go.jp, December 6, 2002).

Chapter V
Consular Affairs

Japan-China Consular Agreement: *
Trajectory from the Shenyang Consulate-General Incident

Introduction

"China detains North Koreans in Japanese Consulate-General?", "Japanese side protests ... requests hand over", "China argues it complied with the convention": headlines of articles that appeared in the newspapers dated May 9, 2002.[1] The outbreak of the Shenyang Consulate-General incident was reported on TV with lively footage, and shocking photographs adorned newspapers and magazines. The government of Japan strongly protested the Chinese government over the application of international law (Vienna Convention on Consular Relations), and the diplomatic authorities of both countries were in sharp conflict. Nevertheless, the Ministry of Foreign Affairs and the Consulate-General received unforgiving criticism from within Japan, and the government's response was taken up severely every day in the Diet.[2] Eight years after this incident, in January 2010, the two foreign ministers exchanged instruments of ratification for the Japan-China Agreement on Consular Relations in Tokyo, which meant the first bilateral consular agreement for Japan in 43 years. In this paper, I will look back on the trajectory of the eight years since the occurrence of the Shenyang Consulate-General Incident, discuss the issues that the Japanese government had to tackle, and clarify what kind of conclusions the bilateral agreement had reached on the issues of international law.

The author was directly involved in the handling of the case, the launch of negotiations on international agreement, and the actual negotiations as the director of the Chinese Division of the Foreign Ministry of Japan at the time of the Shenyang incident and then as the minister of the Japanese embassy in Beijing. However, the views expressed in this paper do not represent the views of the government or the Ministry of Foreign Affairs, except for direct citations such as parliamentary statements and external announcements.

First appearance of the paper: "Japan-China Consular Agreement: Trajectory from the Shenyang Consulate-General Incident", Yuuhikaku, *Jurist*, No. 1402, June, 2015.

I. Shenyang Consulate-General Incident and remaining issues

1 The Case

Around 3:00 p.m. on May 8, 2002, armed police officers of China chased North Korean defectors (a total of five men and women, including infants) who tried to enter the Consulate-General of Japan in Shenyang, the capital of Liaoning Province, China. The incident occurred when the police officers entered the premises without obtaining the consent of the Consulate-General and took the North Koreans away. After the incident, the Japanese government strongly protested against the Chinese side that the actions of the local public security authorities had violated the Vienna Convention on Consular Relations, which stipulated that the consular premises was inviolable, and requested to hand over the five people from a humanitarian point of view. The Chinese side initially said, "(Entry into the Consulate-General) was a measure to ensure the safety of the Japanese premises," and "Chinese response was in accordance with Article 31-2 of the convention, which said that the consent of the head of the consular post may be assumed in case of fire or other disaster requiring prompt protective action." However, three days later, on the night of May 10, it changed its stance and advocated "the Chinese armed police officers had entered the Japanese premises with the consent of the Consulate-General," and "a Consulate-General official had agreed that Chinese public security officials would take five North Koreans and expressed gratitude to the armed police." The Foreign Ministry of Japan dispatched a team headed by the Director-General of the Consular Affairs Bureau from Tokyo to Shenyang to establish the facts, and announced the results of the investigation on May 13. The report clarified again that there was no evidence that the Consulate-General had given consent to the Chinese officials regarding both entry into the premises and the taking of five people involved and requested the Chinese government to solve the problem as soon as possible from the viewpoint of international law and the humanitarian point of view.

In this way, the perceptions of both sides became completely incompatible over the core fact of "whether or not there was consent", and criticism continued between Japan and China. On the other hand, the Japanese government actively worked in order to resolve the treatment of five North Korean defectors, who had started the incident, in a humane way. The Japanese side repeatedly made it clear to the Chinese side that humanitarian demands had priority through high-level diplomatic channels in Tokyo and Beijing, through a Chinese high-level visitor to Japan and through Chinese Foreign Ministers visiting third countries.[3] Finally, at midnight on May 21, the Chinese government agreed to the departure of those five people to a third country, and on the following day, they left for South Korea via an intermediate point.

2. Remaining issues

In responding to the Shenyang Consulate-General Incident, the Government of Japan had consistently requested three points: early handover of the five North Korean defectors, an apology, and a guarantee of recurrence prevention. This was because, regarding a typical case of violation of the Vienna Convention on Consular Relations such as this, it was thought that calm discussions on the issue of state responsibility for international wrongful acts would contribute to the early resolution of the issue.[4]

The International Law Commission had already adopted the final draft articles on Responsibility of States for International Wrongful Acts in 2001, one year before the Shenyang incident, which deals with the breach of an international obligation of a state and reparation for injury. The Japanese side had expected that the final draft would present a guideline in processing a case, like the Shenyang Incident, where "there is a breach of an international obligation by a State when an act of that State is not in conformity with what is required of it by that obligation" (Article 12 of the draft article).[5] "Early handover of the five North Korean defectors" was "restitution, that is, to re-establish the situation which existed before the wrongful act was committed" (Article 35), and "Apologize" was a form of "Satisfaction" (Article 37). The final draft article did not include "guarantee of recurrence prevention" in the Chapter of Reparation for Injury; however, it also stipulated "to offer appropriate assurances and guarantees of non-repetition" as an obligation of the State responsible for an international wrongful act (Article 30). The actual exchange between Japan and China fell into a stalemate at the level of fact recognition, and the situation continued without hope for the calm discussions originally intended by the Japanese government. However, there had always existed the three points of request based upon international law on releasing liability in the background of the Japanese side.

The first request, "early handover of the five North Korean defectors", was a request to return the parties concerned to the situation before the incident, and was a request for "restoration to the original state" in the literal sense. However, from the standpoint of the five North Korean defectors involved in the case, their ultimate goal was not to be admitted to a foreign diplomatic mission, and it was obvious that their purpose was to safely depart to a third country from China, where they would have to live always in fear of being caught as illegal residents. Therefore, even if the Chinese side had handed over five defectors to the Japanese Consulate General in Shenyang at the request of the Japanese government, that would not have solved the problem. In such a case, the Japanese side had to secure the final host country and after that, it would be necessary to obtain the understanding and cooperation of the territorial country, China, regarding their safe departure. Behind the Japanese Government's continuous request to the Chinese side that "the fulfillment of humanitarian demands for the five North Korean defectors is the highest priority," there existed such logical development. In other words, the Japanese side judged that, even if the Chinese side had not actually handed over the five persons concerned to the Japanese side, if safe departure to a third country was permitted, the purpose of the first request, "restoration to the original state," would be realized. Two weeks after the occurrence of the incident, as mentioned above, the Chinese government finally allowed the defectors to leave the country and travel to South Korea via a third country. When their entry into South Korea was safely realized, the purpose of the first of the three requests set by the Japanese government, "early handover of the five North Korean defectors," was also achieved.

As a result, for the Japanese Government there remained two points, those were to receive an "apology" and "guarantee of recurrence prevention" from the Chinese government.

II. Limitations of the Vienna Convention on Consular Relations

1. Divergence from the inviolability of the consular premises

The claims of both Japan and China regarding the Shenyang case differed by 180 degrees at the level of fact recognition of "whether or not there was consent", but both sides used the Vienna Convention on Consular Relations as a basis for justifying their claims. In the process of drafting the convention adopted by the United Nations Conference on Consular Relations in Vienna in 1963, much debate was actually about the inviolability of the consular mission. Is the inviolability of consular missions established as generally as the inviolability of diplomatic missions? Because of the Cold War of the 1960s, mainly communist countries insisted on "general and absolute inviolability" compared with "restrictive inviolability" claimed by the United States, Britain, Japan, etc.[6] Here, I would like to revisit the relevant provisions of the Vienna Convention on Consular Relations, which was adopted after such discussions, in comparison with the Vienna Convention on Diplomatic Relations (adopted in 1961).

(1) Restrictive inviolability

Article 22-1 of the Vienna Convention on Diplomatic Relations stipulates, "The premises of the mission shall be inviolable" and clarifies that the diplomatic missions enjoy general inviolability. On the other hand, Article 31-1 of the Vienna Convention on Consular Relations stipulates, "Consular premises shall be inviolable to the extent provided in this Article" and clarifies the idea that general and unconditional inviolability is not allowed for the consular premises, but that inviolability is permitted only within the limits set by the Convention.

(2) Spatial restrictions

One manifestation of the restrictive inviolability of the consular mission's premises is the restriction on the inviolable space. Article 22-1 of the Vienna Convention on Diplomatic Relations stipulates, "The agents of the receiving State may not enter them, except with the consent of the head of the mission". Therefore, it is clear that inviolability is allowed in all spaces of the mission. On the other hand, the provisions of Article 31-2 of the Vienna Convention on Consular Relations state that "the authorities of the receiving State shall not enter that part of the consular premises which is used exclusively for the purpose of the work of the consular post except with the consent of the head of the consular post or of his designee or of the head of the diplomatic mission of the sending State". Therefore, it is clear that even if it is on the premises of the mission, the part used for purposes other than consular post will not enjoy inviolability. The background of such provision was that in the 1960s, consular missions of the Soviet Union involved non-consular posts such as trade and travel bureau.[7] However, in view of the development of the Shenyang incident, it must be pointed out that this provision leaves ambiguity to give the authorities of the receiving State a basis for unauthorized entry into the premises of the consular mission.

(3) Fire or other disaster requiring prompt protective action

Following the spatial restrictions in (2) above, Article 31-2 of the Vienna Convention on Consular Relations further states that "the consent of the head of the consular post may, however, be assumed in case of fire or other disaster that requires prompt protective action." If a fire breaks out in a foreign consular mission located in the center of a city, there is a high probability that the spread of fire will cause serious loss to the lives and property of the local residents. Therefore, it is natural that, in such a case, the authorities of the receiving State may take prompt protective action. However, it is necessary to consider separately whether such common sense judgment should be stated clearly as an exception to the inviolability of the consular mission. In this regard, the Vienna Convention on Diplomatic Relations remains silent and sticks to a cautious position on restricting, at least in writing, the "inviolability of the premises of the mission". However, by clarifying this point, the Vienna Convention on Consular Relations reiterated that there were restrictions on the inviolability of the premises of consular missions. Also by stipulating "in case of fire or other disaster that requires prompt protective actions", the convention left room for freedom of action on the part of the receiving State Government.[8] As mentioned above, at the beginning of the Shenyang Consulate General Incident, the Ministry of Foreign Affairs of China tried to justify unauthorized entry and taking of the North Korean defectors by using this provision, and from that background, I have to raise doubts about the appropriateness of this exception provision.

(4) Residence of the head of the consular post

The residence of the head of the diplomatic mission (so-called ambassador's residence) is part of the "premises of the mission" under the Vienna Convention on Diplomatic Relations (Article 1(i)) and is included in the inviolable subject. In addition, Article 30 (1) of the Convention stipulates that "the private residence of a diplomatic agent shall enjoy the same inviolability and protection as the premises of the mission," and clarifies that the inviolability also covers the residence of diplomatic staff other than the ambassador. On the other hand, the Vienna Convention on Consular Relations does not have a specific provision on the residence of the head of the consular post and the residence of the consuls, and as a result, it has become clear that the inviolability does not cover those residences.[9] The fact that there are no provisions relating to the Consul General's residence or consul's residence raises a subtle issue in its application to the Shenyang incident. This was because the official residence of the Consul General of Japan in Shenyang existed on the premises of the Consulate General. At the time of the Shenyang incident, the video near the main gate of the Consulate General was repeatedly televised. If one entered the site from that gate and turned to the right, he or she would see the building of the Consul General's official residence, and if one turned to the left, he or she would see the main building (office building). In the case of the Shenyang incident, North Korean defectors (two men) who rushed to the premises after breaking the restraint of the gatekeeper headed for the main building office on the left side and were arrested in the visa waiting room, so the Japanese side could accuse the Chinese authorities that they had infringed the inviolability of consular premises. However, if they were to run to the right from the gate and be seized by the Chinese authority at the Consul General's residence, there might have been no possibility for the Japanese side to protest on the bases of "violation of international law". In such a case, it would be highly questionable whether the Chinese government would have agreed to the safe departure of the five defectors.

2. Preventing recurrence in the face of difficulties

Considering the limitations of the Vienna Convention on Consular Relations mentioned above, it becomes clear that it was extremely difficult to secure the prevention of recurrence of the Shenyang incident by relying solely on the Vienna Convention. For example, at the time of the incident, the scene at the main gate of the Consulate General was reported as a concrete image of the infringement of inviolability of the consular mission by the Chinese authorities. However, if one understood that gate as the gate to the Consul General's official residence, it could have become a facility outside of inviolability. On the third day after the incident, the Chinese government chose to focus on the fact of "with or without consent", so the Japanese and Chinese governments had, at least, a common ground of argument that "if one had entered the premises and taken the defectors without consent, it would have constituted a violation of the Vienna Convention on Consular Relations." However, if the Chinese government had shown a willingness to contend head-on for the evaluation of the Shenyang incident under international law, the argument would have taken a different path. In such a case, the Japanese Government would have to examine several points in detail. For example, the Japanese side had to examine the following points. The spatial restrictions on the inviolability of the consular post (which part of the site was "used exclusively for the purpose of the work of the consular post"). How to treat the exceptions in case of emergency (relationship between prevention of danger of terrorism and "in case of fires or other disaster that requires prompt protective actions"). How to understand the exclusion of the Consul General's residence from the consular premises (it was highly possible that an infringement of inviolability would not be established even if one entered the main gate without permission) etc. It would have been required of the Japanese government to prove strictly which part of the actions of the Chinese authorities was a violation of international law.

In ordinary bilateral relations, there are never many opportunities to be aware of the existence of specific provisions in international conventions, so it can be understood that something very unusual or totaly unexpected is happening if one is aware of the existence of such provisions. Therefore, on the rationality and legitimacy of the provisions of the Convention, it is important to go through verification from practice on whether one can apply them in actual emergencies, and whether the application leads to rational conclusions. Through its application to the specific case of the Shenyang Consulate-General incident, it became clear that the Vienna Convention on Consular Relations had various limitations. In particular, leaving a situation where the inviolability of consular premises was extremely restrictive and ambiguous could mean a great deal of trouble for Japan in case an emergency occurs again between Japan and China. While proceeding with the handling of the Shenyang incident, the concrete path to achieve the remaining task of preventing the recurrence of the infringement of the inviolability of the consular mission and obtaining a guarantee for it from the Chinese government was gradually becoming clear.

III. Start of Consular Cooperation Framework Talks

1. Holding of Japan-China Foreign Ministers' Meeting

2002, when the Shenyang Consulate-General incident occurred, marked the 30th anniversary of the normalization of relations between Japan and China. Just one month before the incident, Li Peng, Chairman of the National People's Congress Standing Committee, had visited Japan (from April 2 to 9), and Prime Minister Koizumi had visited Hainan Province, China, to attend the Boao Forum (April 11-13), and held a meeting with the Premier Zhu Rongji. Prime Minister Koizumi visited Yasukuni Shrine on April 21. The Shenyang incident occurred when the atmosphere between the two countries was tense. Although humanitarian solutions were obtained after two weeks of rigorous exchanges, the remaining issues were by no means small, and the 30th anniversary exchange program was difficult to facilitate without answers to these issues.

The Japan-China Foreign Ministers' Meeting, held in Cha-am, Thailand one month after the incident, became the first step to overcome such tensions between the two countries. On June 19, Foreign Minister Kawaguchi, who attended the Asia Cooperation Dialogue (ACD), had the first Japan-China Foreign Ministers' Meeting after the Shenyang Incident with Tang Jiaxuan, Foreign Minister of China. Minister Kawaguchi pointed out that although the five defectors concerned had left China to a third country, there remained a strong opinion in Japan that the Chinese side had infringed the inviolability of the Consul-General of Japan. Then she proposed to start talks between the diplomatic authorities to prevent the recurrence of such a situation. Minister Tang Jiaxuan also said, "I agree with Minister Kawaguchi's idea that the two countries should keep calm and communicate with each other to prevent the spread of the problem," and agreed to start talks on recurrence prevention. This agreement was reconfirmed at the Japan-China Foreign Ministers' Meeting at the ASEAN Post Ministerial Conference (PMC) held in Brunei in July, and it was decided that the discussions on the framework of consular cooperation would begin. Then, at the first meeting of the Consular Cooperation Framework Talks held in Beijing on August 29, an unexpected statement came out from the Chinese side, which was a turning point in a series of negotiations with China.

2. Chinese government admitting its blame

At the beginning of the talks, the head of the Chinese delegation, the deputy Director-General of the Department of Consular Affairs of the Ministry of Foreign Affairs of China said, "the Chinese side had handled the Shenyang Incident calmly so as not to affect the big picture of bilateral relations. Although both China and Japan may have some responsibility for this incident, the Chinese side dealt with it from the big picture of China-Japan friendship." ... The Chinese side is acknowledging its responsibility for the Shenyang Incident... The author, who was present at the talks, doubted his ears.[10] The problems on the Japanese side regarding the Shenyang Incident had been clear from the beginning. In the investigation results announced on May 13, the Ministry of Foreign Affairs clarified problems such as the lack of awareness of a crisis that existed at the time of the incident, inadequate command system and security system, and on July 5, the Government of Japan announced improvement measures and dispositions of related parties. In this way, the Japanese side admitted that there had been a problem on its own side from the beginning of the incident, but the Chinese side had not acknowledged its own responsibility at all. At the Japan-China Foreign Ministers' Meeting in June, when they agreed to hold a consular cooperation framework consultation, Foreign Minister Kawaguchi stated, "there exists a strong opinion in Japan that the Chinese side has infringed the inviolability of the Consulate General of Japan." In response to the statement, Minister Tang Jiaxuan only said, "China's actions came from a sense of responsibility to protect the safety of the Consulate General, and the consent of the Consulate General's officials had been obtained in advance. Therefore, there is no problem of infringing the so-called inviolability of the Consulate General." The above statement was made in such a situation. The Chinese representative's remarks regarding the Shenyang Incident were short, and did not reveal what kind of responsibility the Chinese government was considering for the incident. However, the Chinese Government, which had not acknowledged any responsibility for the incident at any level since the incident's occurrence on May 8, admitted its blame at the formal talks between Japan and China. The significance of the statement was not small.[11]

I have already pointed out that the "Apology" the Japanese Government requested from the beginning of the Shenyang Incident was a form of "satisfaction" referred to in Article 37 of the Responsibility of States for Internationally wrongful Acts (final draft). Article 37-3 of the final draft stipulates, "Satisfaction shall not take a form humiliating to the responsible State" and indicates that there is a limit to the form of "satisfaction". The remarks made by the Chinese delegation in the Consular Cooperation Framework Talks could not be regarded as an "apology", but they clearly acknowledged their blame at the official level of the Chinese Foreign Ministry. Furthermore, in September following the talks, Chinese Foreign Minister Tang Jiaxuan said to Foreign Minister Kawaguchi, who visited Beijing, "The first round of the Consular Cooperation Framework Talks was held, and I think it was a good start. I hope that the talks will have a substantial effect." These remarks also showed indirectly that the top Chinese diplomat had no objection to the statement by the Chinese delegation at the Talks. Needless to say, these series of remarks by the Chinese side greatly eased the tension that had existed between Japan and China since the incident. After the Japan-China Foreign Ministers' Meeting in September, the Government of Japan was to fully tackle the last issue left by the Shenyang Incident, "securing prevention of recurrence."

IV. Japanese NGO official's detention case and start of negotiations to conclude bilateral agreement

1. Burden of the Vienna Convention

It was clear from the above-mentioned examination that the Vienna Convention needed an adjustment to prevent the recurrence of the Shenyang Incident, but the Japanese Government could not reach a conclusion immediately on whether or not to enter into negotiations to conclude a new bilateral consular agreement with China. Until then, the only consular agreements that Japan had concluded bilaterally were with the United States, the United Kingdom and the Soviet Union, and all of those bilateral agreements were signed before the Vienna Convention came into effect. The Vienna Convention on Consular Relations, drafted by the United Nations International Law Commission and adopted at the United Nations Conference on Consular Relations in Vienna, has already become what can be called general international law. As long as there is already codified general international law in the fields of international relations, we should be inherently cautious to set up different rights and obligations one after another in individual bilateral relations. In fact, at the Consular Cooperation Framework Talks between Japan and China, in addition to legal issues, the two Governments also promoted examination of various specific improvement measures such as establishing an emergency contact route in the event of an emergency and strengthening communication between the consular mission and local police authorities.[12] However, the problem was that only applying the Vienna Convention, which has various limitations, could not secure the prevention of recurrence of the Shenyang Incident, and there was an urgent need to formulate more fundamental recurrence prevention measures.

2. Detention case where there was no consular notification

On October 30, 2002, a detention case of a Japanese NGO official occurred in Dalian, Liaoning Province, China. On that morning, Hiroshi Kato, the secretary-general of the North Korean Refugee Relief Fund, and a Japanese student interpreter suddenly disappeared in Dalian during their visit.[13] Upon contact from the fund, the Ministry of Foreign Affairs of Japan also sought to communicate with the Chinese government and local authorities, and requested to release the two men if the Chinese authorities were detaining them.[14] However, no reliable information came from the Chinese government, and finally on the night of November 5, when the anxiety of the people involved reached its peak, the Ministry of Foreign Affairs of China made a notification to the Japanese Embassy in Beijing. The notification said that Chinese authorities had detained secretary-general Kato and a Japanese student interpreter on October 30 on suspicion of violating the Foreigner Immigration Control Act, and that secretary-general Kato would be deported on the following day, November 6.[15] All the people concerned were relieved that the missing person was confirmed to be safe, but the question arose about the initial response from the Chinese side. The Chinese government and local authorities had avoided clear response to repeated inquiries from the Embassy and Consulate-General of Japan for almost a week.[16] Article 36 of the Vienna Convention on Consular Relations obliges the receiving State to inform the consular post of the sending State without delay if a national of the sending State was arrested or committed to prison or to custody or was detained and if that national requested such notification. If secretary-general Kato had requested such consular notification to the Japanese Embassy or Consulate-General during the period of detention, the Chinese government, which ignored such request and did not make contact with the Japanese side for almost a week, would surely be criticized for violation of the Vienna Convention.

Secretary-general Kato, who returned to Japan by deportation on November 6, visited the Ministry of Foreign Affairs on November 7 and revealed that he had requested three times for consular notification to the Japanese Embassy during the period of detention by the Chinese authorities, but that his requests were never heard.[17] On the other hand, the Chinese Ministry of Foreign Affairs said at a press conference on the same day, November 7, "The facts of the crime are clear"; "although Mr. Kato did not want to report to the Japanese side, the Chinese side contacted the Japanese Embassy", and denied the secretary-general's allegations head-on.[18] The Japanese Government made a request to the Chinese side to clarify the facts, but the Chinese side did not change their explanation that "there had been no request for a consular notification."

It was a desperate feeling of déjà vu that came over the author who dealt with the case as the director of the China Division of the Ministry of Foreign Affairs at that time. Despite the provisions of the Vienna Convention (Article 36, 1 (b)) being quite clear, if both parties claim conflicting facts, the Convention does not provide any protection for foreigners. In the Shenyang Incident, "whether or not there was consent" was disputed, and in the case of the detention of a Japanese NGO official, "whether or not there was a request for consular notification" was the focus. In each case, the truth was put into a kind of black box, the parties claimed the opposite fact recognition, and international law became silenced before those claims.

The protection of Japanese nationals is a top priority for Japanese diplomatic and consular missions abroad. Human exchange between Japan and China has increased dramatically, with a record 2.93 million travelers in 2002. With so many Japanese visiting China on a daily basis, the Ministry of Foreign Affairs of Japan could not overlook the fact that consular notification could not be secured when Japanese were detained in China. What were the obstacles to changing this situation? What was revealed during the examination was once again the limits inherent in the Vienna Convention.

The focus of the facts that had been put into a black box this time was "whether or not there had been a request for consular notification". The reason why the presence or absence of this request influenced the conclusion was because Article 36-1 (b) of the Vienna Convention had adopted the "request pre-positional principle". However, the draft of the Convention drawn up by the United Nations International Law Commission had taken an exact opposite position, which was an "automatic notification," obligating the receiving State to make a consular notification without the need for a detainee's request.[19] In this regard, neither the British-Japanese Consular Convention (effective in 1965) nor the Japanese-Soviet Union Consular Convention (effective in 1967) adopted a request pre-positional principle. Those Conventions obligated a consular notification "when detained … without delay" or "immediately when arrested or detained otherwise". If a Japanese detention case like the one that occurred in Dalian had occurred in Liverpool or Khabarovsk, there would be no dispute over whether or not there was a request, and the consular notification would have been made immediately and without delay, and the protection of Japanese nationals would have been secured. In China, visited by an overwhelmingly large number of Japanese people compared to Russia and the United Kingdom, there was no level of protection like in the UK and Russia. This conclusion was unacceptable to the Government of Japan.

3. Foreigners' crime problem in Japan

In response to the Shenyang Incident and the detention case of a Japanese NGO official, the perceptions in the Government of Japan were being unified that in order to formulate fundamental recurrence prevention measures for these series of cases, it was necessary to supplement and expand the relevant provisions of the Vienna Convention. In addition, it was the growing social concern on crime committed by foreigners visiting Japan that promoted this unified perception to the actual negotiations to conclude a bilateral agreement.

The number of foreigners' crimes in Japan during 2002 reached a record high of 34,746, and it was pointed out that the number of arrests of violent criminals also increased. In addition, according to the status of arrests by nationality, China accounted for a high proportion of 12,667 cases (composition ratio 36.5%) and 6,487 people (40.0% of the same).[20]

At that time, there was a significant gap between Japan's and China's perceptions on this crime issue. The most serious part of this perception gap was the fact that the Chinese government, not only the Ministry of Foreign Affairs but also the public security authorities, did not grasp the situation that so many Chinese citizens were getting arrested in Japan. Not many Chinese detained in Japan wished to report to their consular post. As a result, it was possible for a criminal to return to China without being noticed by those around him, and sometimes even to return home as a successful person. In China, the issuance of ordinary passports and immigration control are handled by the Public Security line (Ministry of Public Security in the central Government, Public Security Agencies at provincial-level, and Public Security Bureaus at city-level). Therefore, if the Japanese side can communicate to the Chinese authorities on specific facts of all criminal cases in a proper way, it can be expected to have a certain effect in terms of preventing the return of those who have committed crimes in Japan. The mandatory consular notification (reporting all cases of Chinese crimes in Japan to the Chinese authorities) was expected to provide an institutional guarantee for the realization of this purpose.[21]

4. Start of negotiations for a bilateral consular agreement

In January 2003, the Government of Japan held the second round meeting of the Consular Cooperation Framework Talks in Tokyo, and proposed to obligate consular notification in addition to preventing the recurrence of the Shenyang Incident. The Chinese side responded that both could be fully dealt with in a bilateral consular agreement. Based upon the results of this discussion and the examinations within the government departments, the Japanese Government decided to seek a new agreement with China in the field of consular relations from the perspectives of both protecting its own citizens and cooperation in the field of public security. Foreign Minister Kawaguchi, who visited Beijing in April, 2003, communicated this policy to Li Zhaoxing, who had just become the Foreign Minister of China; and at the Japan-China Foreign Ministers' Meeting, it was agreed to start negotiations to conclude bilateral consular agreement.

The first round of negotiations on the bilateral consular agreement took place in the same month, late April 2003 in Beijing, where the entire city had calmed down from the spread of Severe Acute Respiratory Syndrome (SARS). After that, in the summer of 2004, harassment of Japanese supporters and damage to embassy vehicles occurred in the Soccer Asia Cup, and in the spring of 2005, which marked the 60th anniversary of the end of the Japan-China war, protests against Japan continued in various parts of China, targeting Japanese missions and companies. There were a series of violent incidents that made the Japanese side realize fully that there was an urgent need to protect Japanese nationals and to establish the inviolability of consular posts in China. On the other hand, the general atmosphere of bilateral relations also affected working level discussions. Because the Chinese side strongly opposed Prime Minister Koizumi's visit to the Yasukuni Shrine, the negotiations on the bilateral consular agreement were suspended for two years from June 2005 to April 2007. The realization of the substantive consensus on the Japan-China Consular Agreement was at the seventh round of negotiations in March 2008, two months before President Hu Jintao's visit to Japan, and it was five years after the start of the negotiations.

V. Conclusion of the Japan-China Consular Agreement

Here, I would like to examine what conclusions Japan and China have made on each of the issues mentioned so far, in line with the contents of the Japan-China Consular Agreement.

1. Relationship with the Vienna Convention on Consular Relations

When creating a bilateral consular agreement between Japan and China, the first thing that had to be organized was the relationships with the Vienna Convention on Consular Relations. This was because it was necessary to answer questions such as whether the conclusion of the new bilateral agreement would prevent Japanese living in China from obtaining the protection stipulated in the Vienna Convention. In this regard, the Government of Japan had decided to find an answer within the Vienna Convention itself. That is Article 73-2 of the Vienna Convention, which states "Nothing in the present Convention shall preclude States from concluding international agreements confirming or supplementing or expanding or amplifying the provisions thereof." By referring to and quoting this provision of the Vienna Convention, it is clarified that the purpose of this Agreement is to confirm, supplement, expand and amplify the Vienna Convention. Also, by clearly stipulating that "Matters not expressly regulated by the present Agreement shall continue to be governed by the Vienna Convention," it was shown that the Vienna Convention and the Bilateral Agreement would complement each other and support each other to establish a new framework for the consular relations between the two countries (Article 12 of the Agreement).

In the discussion on the Vienna Convention, I would like to introduce a strange exchange that took place and that made us realize the history of 40 years from 1963. For drafting this Agreement, there existed a basic idea that only special provisions applicable between Japan and China (strengthening inviolability, mandatory consular notification, etc.) should be stipulated, and that the rest should be based on the Vienna Convention. On the other hand, there also existed a common understanding that we should avoid a situation where, in the event of an emergency, the officials of both countries had to look up both texts of the Vienna Convention and Bilateral Agreement to find out the right rule to be applied. Therefore, the same provisions (like definition clauses (Article 1)) were also set as in the Vienna Convention, but the Chinese draft presented at the negotiation was different from the official text of the Vienna Convention. The Japanese side, of course, took the position that it was not possible to accept a definition different from the Vienna Convention, but the Chinese side responded that they could not understand the counter-argument of the Japanese side. During the negotiations, it became clear that the Chinese text of the Vienna Convention complies with the rhetorical law of the Republic of China, which represented China at the United Nations in 1963, and its old-fashioned writing was far from modern Chinese.[22] On the Japanese side, if the meaning of each article did not differ from the provisions of the Vienna Convention, there was no strong opinion on how to write Chinese as a language. Therefore, the Chinese text of the Agreement became modern Chinese on the one hand, and it was also made clear that the English text would prevail in case of divergence of interpretation among the three equally authentic texts of Japanese, Chinese and English on the other.

2. Inviolability of the Consular Mission (Article 6)

(1) Stipulating General Inviolability

Regarding the nature of the inviolability of the consular premises, it was stipulated squarely "Consular premises shall be inviolable" (Article 6-1 of the Agreement), removing the restriction in the Vienna Convention (Article 31-1) "to the extent provided in this Article". As a result, the same "General Inviolability" as the diplomatic mission's premises became admitted to the consular premises of the two countries.

(2) Removal of Spatial Restrictions

This Agreement also removed the restrictions on the inviolable space. The Vienna Convention (Article 31-2), by stating that "The authorities of the receiving State shall not enter that part of the consular premises which is used exclusively for the purpose of the consular post", admitted that there was a part of the consular premises where the authorities of the receiving State could enter freely. However, through the negotiation, the Japanese side sought to close such a "hole" in the Japan-China Agreement, and finally stipulated "The authorities of the receiving State shall not enter the consular premises except with the consent..." without any spatial exceptions (Article 6-2 of the Agreement).

(3) Removal of references to fires and other emergency disasters

This Agreement also removed the reference to "fires or other disaster requiring prompt protective action", which the Vienna Convention raised as an example of permitting the entry of the receiving State authorities (Article 31-2). At an early stage of the Shenyang Incident, the Chinese Ministry of Foreign Affairs argued to justify unauthorized entry based upon this provision. The Japanese side was concerned about leaving such a clause as it would result in granting the authorities of the receiving State far greater freedom of action than necessary. On the other hand, this did not mean that the receiving State cannot take any action in the event of a fire at a consular premises. As with the Vienna Convention on Diplomatic Relations, it is natural that the authorities of the receiving State can take measures to protect the lives and property of the local residents, such as preventing the spread of fire.[23]

(4) Residence of the head of the consular mission

For a consular mission such as the Japanese Consulate-General in Shenyang, where the building of the consulate-general and the residence of the consul-general were located on the same site, the silence of the Vienna Convention on the residence of the head of the consular mission gave great concern about the possibility of receiving State authorities entering the site without permission. At the time of the negotiations between Japan and China, there was no objection to the idea that the Consul-General's residence and the residence of the Consuls should be granted the same inviolability and protection as the consular premises, but there were some choices in the way of writing. One was that, as the Vienna Convention on Diplomatic Relations, the definition clause would include the residence of the head of the mission in the "premises of the mission", and provide that the private residence of an agent shall enjoy the same inviolability and protection as the premises of the mission. Adopting such provisions did not differ in the degree of inviolability and protection, but did result in a clear distinction under the Agreement between the residence of the head of the mission and the staff's private residence.[24] On the other hand, from the perspective of protection for the consular mission, such a distinction was essentially unnecessary, and by describing the consular officer's residence as a "private residence," it gave the impression of lowering its status further. In preparing this Agreement, the Japanese side aimed for clearer and simpler provisions, and finally stipulated, in the clause on the inviolability of the consular mission (Article 6), "The residence of a consular officer shall enjoy the same inviolability and protection as the consular premises" (Article 6-5).

3. Mandatory consular notification (Article 8)

(1) Elimination of pre-request requirements

What had become clear from the detention case of a Japanese NGO official was an institutional flaw in the Vienna Convention, which adopted the pre-request principle for consular notification. Even if a Japanese person in the arrest / detention stage made a request for a consular notification under the Vienna Convention, if the receiving State authorities denied that fact, he/she would not be able to enjoy the protection under the Convention. Therefore, in the provisions relating to consular notification, the elimination of this pre-request requirement was the first priority. As a result of the discussion, in order to stipulate clearly that the consular notification would not depend on the presence or absence of such a request, we finally agreed on the following text. "If a national of the sending State,…, is arrested or …is detained in any other manner,…, the competent authorities of the receiving State shall…inform the consular post, irrespective of whether he or she so requests" (Article 8-1(b)).

In addition, as a result of such provision, all cases of Chinese arrested in Japan would be reported to Chinese consular agencies (embassies, consulates) without asking whether or not there is a request from the person. This would make it possible for the relevant authorities in China (especially the public security authorities that issue passports and manage immigration control) to grasp the status of these crimes in detail. It is expected that this provision would have a certain effect in preventing the return of those arrested in Japan back to Japan.

(2) "Without delay but not later than four days"

After ensuring the obligatory consular notification, the deadline for notification was included in order to make much prompter notification. Among the bilateral consular conventions concluded by Japan, the United Kingdom-Japan Convention only stipulates that notifications will be made "without delay" and does not mention the deadline for notification. On the other hand, while the Japan-Soviet Union Convention stipulates "immediately" in the text of the Convention (Article 32), the Protocol states "notification to consular posts ... within a period of one to three days at the latest, depending on the status of means of communication. In addition, the Exchange of Notes stipulates that in the case of a violation of territorial waters regulations in the northwestern Pacific, "notification must be done within ten days from the time of arrest or detention."

There are also various precedents on this point in China's national practice, for example, the China-Russia Convention (effective in 2003) stipulates "within 3 working days". The US-China Convention (effective in 1982) stipulates "within 4 days" and the China-Italy Convention (effective in 1991) stipulates "within 7 days". However, the China-India Convention, the China-Pakistan Convention, the China-Canada Agreement, etc. only have qualitative provisions such as "without delay" or "immediately", and do not stipulate a specific deadline for notification.[25] The Japanese government had approached negotiations with the stance that, as long as the bilateral agreement with China stipulates a mandatory notification, the deadline for notification should be set specifically and as short as possible.

In the discussion between Japan and China, the Japanese side pointed out the case of the US-China Convention signed in 1980, and compared the communication situation in China in the early 1980s (where the spread of fixed telephones was delayed) and the present (the world's leading telecommunications powerhouse with mobile phone and Internet connection). The Japanese side argued that if it was possible to inform the consular post within 4 days in the early 1980s, now in the 21st century, even a notification within 3 or 2 days must be completely possible. However, the Chinese side argued that the number of foreigners visiting China had been limited in the early 1980s, and the number of cities open to foreigners had been extremely limited, so it was easy to grasp cases related to foreigners. On the other hand, it is now more difficult to find a place that is not open to foreigners except for Tibet, and foreigners are actually visiting inland and remote villages all over the country. Furthermore, from Japan, there are more than 2 million visitors to China annually, and under such circumstances, it is difficult to maintain the deadline for notification "within 4 days" stipulated in the US-China Convention in the early 1980s. Then, the Chinese side claimed that "within 5 days or 7 days" was appropriate.

In the end, the debate between Japan and China reached a conclusion to make the notification "within 4 days". Behind this conclusion had existed the judgement of ICJ in 2004 on the "Avena and Other Mexican Nationals" case in which Mexico filed a lawsuit against the United States in the International Court of Justice over the issue of consular notification.[26] In this case, the International Court of Justice ruled that the consular notification made within five days (three working days) after the arrest was deemed to have been reported "without delay" in accordance with Article 36-1 (b) of the Vienna Convention. The deadline for notification "within 4 days", which was adopted by the Japan-China Agreement, was found to be consistent with this ruling.

(3) Dealing with the peculiarities of Japanese-Chinese consular matters

The Japan-China Consular Agreement also includes provisions that correspond to the peculiarities of consular cases in China, specifically, the fact that the North Korean defectors case includes an element of protection for Japanese nationals. Behind this aspect was the North Korean Home Returning Project for Koreans living in Japan from the 1950s to the 1980s. Among the people who went to North Korea during this return movement were more than 6,000 Japanese nationals (Japanese wives and children). Such Japanese people were also included in the cases of North Korean defectors handled by the Embassy in Beijing, the Consulate General in Shenyang, and others. Those who had lived in North Korea for decades under severe conditions and defected from North Korea, of course, did not have any documents to prove that they were Japanese nationals, and some had even forgotten the Japanese language. In the eyes of the Chinese authorities, these people were nothing more than illegal immigrants who disturbed the public security, but in the eyes of Japanese people, they were Japanese citizens who had left the land of North Korea, dreaming of returning to their home and crossing the Yalu River for their lives. They are, of course, a citizen of the sending State who can receive the appropriate protection under the Japan-China Agreement. Having no certificate of being Japanese or not understanding the Japanese language should not become a reason to hinder the enjoyment of protection as a Japanese citizen. In this agreement, specific provisions were set in order to deal with such actual consular matters.

One of them is Article 8-1 (b). This article stipulates that a national of the sending State "including a person who claims to be a national of the sending State, unless proved otherwise" would be subject to the mandatory consular notification. Even if the Chinese authorities arrest a Japanese defector from North Korea, if he or she claims to be Japanese, one will be treated as a Japanese citizen even if one does not have anything to prove one's identity and the consular notification will be made. In addition, Article 8-1 (a) stipulates, "The receiving

State shall not prevent nationals of the sending State from contacting with consular officers, or from entering consular premises." This is a special provision to prevent similar incidents from occurring for the Japanese people, based on the experience of the Shenyang Incident where the Chinese armed police tried to prevent North Korean defectors from entering the Consul General. This "nationals of the sending State", of course, include Japanese nationals who had once participated in the Home Returning Project and moved to North Korea.

4. Coming into effect of the Japan-China Agreement

The Japanese Diet unanimously approved the Agreement on Consular Relations between Japan and the People's Republic of China at its 171st session in July 2009, and in China, the National People's Congress Standing Committee ratified it in February of the same year.[27] The exchange of instruments of ratification took place in Tokyo on January 17, 2010, and the Agreement entered into force on February 16, on the 30th day of the exchange. Eight years after the Shenyang Consulate General Incident, the Government of Japan had realized the last remaining task, "securing prevention of recurrence," with the conclusion of a bilateral Consular Agreement, which would bring the full consular protection to Japanese people staying in China and also would be expected to have a certain effect on public security in Japan.

Epilogue

The story goes back to the early 1990s when I was working at the Japanese Embassy in Beijing as a first secretary. One weekend, when I headed to the Embassy, a young man stood in front of the gate and dimly looked at the Embassy. Looking at him while passing by, I realized he was one of the armed police officers who greeted the Embassy staff in front of the gate in the mornings and evenings. Not in the usual uniform, the off-duty plain clothes showed him to be surprisingly young. When I asked what happened, he said he would return to his hometown of Sichuan tomorrow due to a transfer. He told me that he had protected the gates of various embassies in Beijing, but because the Japanese Embassy was the longest standing, he came to see the place before leaving Beijing. The young man looked up at the Embassy shining in the sunset, and the Rising Sun Flag was swaying high on the pole.

The armed police officers who entered the Consulate-General and took the North Korean defectors at the Shenyang Incident must have been upset and impatient that the defectors had rushed through the gate they had been guarding. They must also have thought that they had to protect the Consul-General of Japan. Their actions were targets of criticism under international law, and that was the reason why the Japanese Government strongly protested against the Chinese government as described above. However, if there are ambiguities in international law, and such ambiguities have led them to act against international law, the same kind of incident will be repeated unless the cause is removed. Negotiations on the Japan-China Consular Agreement have sought to remove such ambiguities of international law and fill the gap. With the conclusion of the Agreement, I sincerely hope that the young Chinese officers who guard the Japanese Embassy and Consulates will return home with pride again.

Notes

* For the text of the Japan-China Consular Agreement, refer to the Ministry of Foreign Affairs website (www.mofa.go.jp).
1 *Asahi Shimbun*, morning and evening edition, May 9, 2002.
2 "The 154th House of Representatives Minutes No. 32". "The 154th House of Councilors Meeting Minutes No. 23".
3 Prime Minister Junichiro Koizumi and Foreign Minister Kawaguchi made requests to Hu Qili, the Vice President of the National Political Consultative Conference, who was visiting Japan at that time. Vice Foreign Minister Sugiura made a request to the Foreign Minister Tang Jiaxuan in East Timor. Foreign Minister Kawaguchi made a request to Zhao Qizheng, the Minister of the State Council Information Office, who was visiting Japan at that time.
4 Toshiya Ueki, "The Case of the Consulate-General of Japan in Shenyang and International Law", *Law School*, No. 263, Yuhikaku, August 2002, pp. 58-64.

5   For the Japanese translation of "Responsibility of State for Internationally Wrongful Acts", see Yoshiro Matsui (ed), *Basic Documents of International Law 2010*, Toshindo, 2010, pp. 160-165.

6   Kisaburo Yokota, *International Law on Consular Relations*, Yuhikaku, 1974, pp. 201-222.

7   Kisaburo Yokota, *International Law on Consular Relations*, Yuhikaku, 1974, p. 203.

8   As an exception to the inviolability of the consular premises, it was a joint proposal by the United Kingdom, Japan and others that requested the explicit provision of fires and other emergency disasters. Kisaburo Yokota, *International Law on Consular Relations*, Yuhikaku, 1974, pp. 207-209.

9   Kisaburo Yokota, *International Law on Consular Relations*, Yuhikaku, 1974, pp. 211, 219.

10   "China acknowledges responsibility ... about taking defectors ... at Consular talks", morning edition of the *Yomiuri Shimbun*, August 29, 2002. "China says 'both countries are responsible' ... Japan-China talks, no specific details", *Tokyo Shimbun* morning edition, August 29, 2002.

11   "The 156th House of Representatives Foreign Affairs Committee Minutes No. 8", pp. 3-4.

12   "Proposal of recurrence prevention measures in response to the Shenyang incident ... Consular talks between Japan and China", *Mainichi Shimbun* morning edition, August 29, 2002. "First talks in Beijing, Japan-China Consular Departments ... Measures to prevent recurrence of the Shenyang incident", *Asahi Shimbun* morning edition, August 29, 2002.

13   "After entering China, missing ... Secretary of the North Korean defectors support organization", *Yomiuri Shimbun* morning edition, November 2, 2002.

14   "The 155th House of Councilors Foreign Affairs and Defense Committee Minutes No. 2", p. 6. "The 155th House of Representatives Foreign Affairs Committee Minutes No. 4", p. 4.

15   "Supporter of North Korean defectors / Missing Japanese are detained ... Deported from China today", "Liberation of NGO for North Korean defectors ... Japanese family relieved", *Yomiuri Shimbun* morning edition, November 6, 2002.

16   "We will protest if the Vienna Convention is violated ... Suggested by the Ministry of Foreign Affairs", *Asahi Shimbun* morning edition, November 7, 2002.

17   "I asked to contact the Embassy three times during custody ... NGO secretary", *Yomiuri Shimbun* morning edition, November 8, 2002.

18 "Mr. Kato's crime, obvious facts ... China's Ministry of Foreign Affairs argues", *Asahi Shimbun* morning edition, November 8, 2002.

19 It was Japan, Canada and others that submitted amendment proposals from the standpoint of "pre-request requirement" at the Vienna Conference on Consular Relations. Kisaburo Yokota, *International Law on Consular Relations*, Yuhikaku, 1974, pp. 260-277.

20 "National Police Agency International Organizational Crime Countermeasures, Characteristics of Foreigners' Crimes from Statistics", "Current Situation of Foreigners' Crimes (during 2002)" (www.npa.go.jp/kokusai2/toc.main.htm).

21 Council of Ministers for Crime Countermeasures, "Action Plan for Realizing a Crime-Resistant Society ... Aiming for the Revival of Japan as the Safest Country in the World" (www.kantei.go.jp, December 2003).

22 The Chinese text of the Vienna Convention on Consular Relations can be found at the United Nations Treaty Collection (http://treaties.un.org).

23 Kisaburo Yokota, *International Law on Foreign Relations*, Yuhikaku, 1963, pp. 212-240.

24 Kisaburo Yokota, *International Law on Foreign Relations*, Yuhikaku, 1963, pp. 307-314.

25 See www.gqb.gov.cn, www.voyage.gc.ca and www.chinaruslaw.com.

26 International Court of Justice, "Case Concerning Avena and other Mexican Nationals (Mexico v. United States of America), judgment of 31 March 2004, para 97 (www.icj-cij.org).

27 Xinhuanet, "Decision on Ratification by the National People's Congress Standing Committee of Consular Agreement between People's Republic of China and Japan" (http://news.xinhuanet.com, February 28, 2009). "The 171st Diet Minutes of the House of Councilors No. 35".

Chapter VI
Human Rights of a Hijacker

CAAC Flight Hijacking Incident

Introduction

On the afternoon of December 16, 1989, a hijacking incident occurred. A CAAC (Civil Aviation Administration of China) jumbo
jet from Beijing was hijacked on the way to Shanghai and made an
emergency landing at Fukuoka Airport. The injured criminal, Zhang
Zhenhai, stated that he had participated in a demonstration in the
Tiananmen Square Incident in June of the same year and he had decided to escape from the country after being arrested, claiming that it
was a hijacking for political purposes. How should the Japanese government deal with the unprecedented situation of a hijacked foreign
aircraft flying into Japan? What were the norms set by international
law regarding the terrorist act of hijacking? How should we understand the relationship with domestic law that sets out the principle of
non-extradition of political prisoners? As the case posed numerous
challenges to the government, the people involved started to put all
their efforts into reaching the best resolution. Mr. KOMATSU Ichiro,
the director of the Legal Affairs Division of the Treaty Bureau of the
Ministry of Foreign Affairs at that time, played a central role in the
legal handling of the case.

First appearance of the paper: "Hijacking Incident of a Civil
Aviation Administration of China Flight", in: Shunji Yanai, Shinya
Murase (eds), *Putting International Law into Practice: In Memory of
Ambassador Ichiro Komatsu*, Shinzansha, June 2015.

1. Occurrence of an incident

The second Tiananmen Square Incident that occurred in 1989 is still a mystery. Following the sudden death of the former General Secretary Hu Yaobang (April 15, 1989), who lost his position in 1987, a large number of young people, mainly students, held a memorial rally and gathered at Tiananmen Square. On the night of April 21, more than 100,000 students and citizens demonstrated at Tiananmen Square for democratization. The occupation of Tiananmen Square by students and citizens did not end even after the arrival of Gorbachev, General Secretary of the Communist Party of the Soviet Union in Beijing (May 15), who visited China to announce the end of the China-Russia conflict. The welcome ceremony at Tiananmen Square was canceled and several events were forced to change venues. The Chinese Communist Party leadership awaited the return of General Secretary Gorbachev and issued martial law in Beijing on May 19, and from the night of June 3, the People's Liberation Army troops were put into Tiananmen Square and forcibly eliminated students and citizens. After that, it is said that a mass arrest was carried out against the persons involved in the case.

In the afternoon of December 16 of the same year, when the memory of the second Tiananmen Square Incident was still fresh, the CAAC (Civil Aviation Administration of China) Jumbo Flight 981 (223 crewmembers and passengers) from Beijing to New York was hijacked on the way to Shanghai. At the request of the hijacker, the aircraft entered Korean territorial air and requested to land at Seoul Gimpo International Airport. However, the South Korean government, which had no diplomatic relations with China at that time, refused. At a point 96 km south of Jeju Island, the South Korean air force was dispatched to scramble. Because the jumbo jet was running out of fuel, Captain Xue Renshan changed course over Jeju Island without notifying the hijacker and made an emergency landing at Fukuoka Airport at 2:52 p.m. with permission. After landing, the crew opened the emergency exit door at the rear of the aircraft. The crew told the hijacker Zhang Zhenhai that "this is Seoul", showed him the opened exit door, and pushed the criminal from behind. Zhang

Zhenhai suffered a serious injury (a broken hip and leg) and was admitted to a hospital in Fukuoka City. There were no injuries to the crew or passengers.[1]

On the same day, at 3:00 p.m., the government of Japan set up the "CAAC Flight Hijacking Response Headquarters" headed by Chief Cabinet Secretary Mme. Moriyama at the Prime Minister's Office, and began studying countermeasures.

2. Issues

(1) International law on hijacking

International law on hijacking and aviation safety is the earliest developed field in a series of terrorist treaties. The "Convention on Offenses and Certain Other Acts Committed on Board Aircraft (Tokyo Convention)" (September 1963, Tokyo) established crimes on an aircraft and the authority of the captain. The "Convention for the Suppression of Unlawful Seizure of Aircraft (Hague Convention)" (December 1970, The Hague)" stipulated heavy punishment for hijacking, jurisdiction setting and extradition, etc. In addition, the "Convention for the Suppression of Unlawful Acts against the Safety of Civil Aviation (Montreal Convention)" (September 1971, Montreal) stipulated heavy punishment for aircraft destruction, jurisdiction setting and extradition, etc. As of 1989, all of these three conventions were in force for Japan. Also in Japan, the "Law on Punishment of Hijacking and other acts" was enacted in 1970, which provided legal foundation to implement those hijacking-related international conventions.

International law related to terrorism continued to expand spatially to the ocean ("Convention for the Suppression of Unlawful Acts against the Safety of Maritime") and continental shelves ("Protocol for the Suppression of Unlawful Acts against the Safety of Fixed Platforms Located on the Continental Shelf"). It also expanded its coverage on terrorism ("Convention on the Prevention and Punishment of Crimes against Internationally Protected Persons, including Diplomatic Agents"). Further, the "Convention against the Taking of

Hostages", "Convention on the Making of Plastic Explosives for the Purpose of Detection", "International Convention for the Suppression of Terrorist Bombings", "International Convention for the Suppression of the Financing of Terrorism", "International Convention for the Suppression of Acts of Nuclear Terrorism". Today, it has led to the formation of a genre in the field of international law.[2] However, in 1989, only a few terrorist treaties existed outside of aviation. Therefore, the relationship between acts of terrorism and political crimes became a major issue within the Japanese government when considering and responding to the incident.

Those international conventions related to terrorism have a pattern that stipulates certain acts as criminal acts under the convention, obliges the State party to punish them, stipulates the extradition of the criminal, and obliges State party to punish the criminal if the party does not extradite them. This is because those conventions have been created with the aim of extinguishing sanctuaries for terrorists through such a framework and ensuring that terrorists are punished wherever they go. Although recent treaties often explicitly state that such acts of terrorism should not be recognized as "political crimes" (Article 11 of the Convention on Terrorist Bombings, Article 14 of the Convention on Financing of Terrorism, Article 15 of the Convention on Nuclear Terrorism), as of 1989, such "denial of political criminality" was not clearly stated. On the one hand, Japan's Extradition Law stipulates the restriction on extradition, that is, the provision that "in case of a political crime" one cannot be "extradited" and on the other, the international conventions stipulate the principle of "extradite, or punish". Since the hijacker, Zhang Zhenhai, had suggested involvement in the Tiananmen Square Incident from the beginning, how to deal with the relationship between the hijacking act and the "political aspect" claimed by the hijacker, became the biggest issue in handling the case.

(2) Other issues

Contention of jurisdiction. In 1989, both Japan and China were already parties to the Hague Convention, and the criminal jurisdiction of China, which was the registered country of the CAAC aircraft, and

Japan, which was the landing country of the aircraft, competed (Article 4(a) and Article 4(b) of the Convention). As mentioned above, "Law on Punishment of Hijacking and other acts" had been enacted in Japan, so it was theoretically possible to carry out criminal trials in Japan. The Convention did not stipulate the superiority or inferiority of competing jurisdiction, but only the principle of "extradite, or punish."

Handling of aircraft and passengers. Article 9 of the Hague Convention provided that the Contracting States "shall take all appropriate measures to restore control of the aircraft to its lawful commander" and "shall facilitate the continuation of the journey of the passengers and crew as soon as practicable". These articles provided guidelines for the response of Japan, which was a State party to the Convention.

Inspection of the aircraft and interviews with crew and passengers. In considering the final handling of the criminal, it was essential for Japan, as the landing country of the hijacked aircraft, to inspect the aircraft as necessary for the investigation and to interview the crew and passengers. On this point, the Japanese government needed to get cooperation from the Chinese side.

(3) Exchange between Japan and China

The exchange between Japan and China at the stage of the incident had not been made public yet. It was only reported in the form of reports[3] and memoirs.[4] Mr. Tanino, the Director-General of the Asian Affairs Bureau of the Minister of Foreign Affairs of Japan invited Mr. Tang Jiaxuan, the Minister at the Chinese Embassy in Tokyo (later the Foreign Minister of China and now the president of the China-Japan Friendship Association) to the Foreign Ministry, and then Ambassador Yang Zhenya had a telephone discussion with Chief Cabinet Secretary Moriyama at midnight. Ambassador Yang Zhenya wrote in his memoirs that he told Chief Cabinet Secretary Moriyama, that on the premise the criminal's wife and children, passengers and crew would return to China on that CAAC flight, the Chinese side would spare no effort in cooperating with the Japanese police authorities' investigation on board.

3. Policy decision

In response to the CAAC Flight Hijacking Incident, the Japanese government decided to (1) waive jurisdiction over the criminal in accordance with the Hague Convention and begin domestic legal proceedings to extradite the criminal to China, and (2) return the aircraft and passengers and crew to China as soon as the inspections and interviews necessary for the investigation were completed. At 10:20 p.m. on the same day, Deputy Chief Cabinet Secretary Ishihara announced this decision at the Prime Minister's Office.

As mentioned above, under the Hague Convention, both the registered country of the hijacked aircraft and the landing country of the aircraft have jurisdiction over the case. However, it was clear from the beginning that it would be extremely difficult to conduct all investigations, prosecutions, and trials in Japan when the aircraft, the criminal and the crew were all Chinese nationals and most of the passengers were Chinese. In addition, if a trial were to be held in Japan, it would be necessary to keep the aircraft, crew and passengers in Japan for a certain period in order to ensure thorough investigation. It must have been difficult for the Japanese government to choose not to respond to the request under the Convention to restore control of the aircraft to the captain and to facilitate the prompt continuation of the trip in order to exercise jurisdiction in its own country.

Furthermore, at the press conference on that night, Deputy Chief Cabinet Secretary Ishihara said, "We gave priority to the Japan-China friendship after comprehensively judging the case and the relationship between Japan and China."[5] He also revealed that in addition to the legal aspects of the case, consideration was given from a political point of view that China, which had deteriorating relations with the West after the Tiananmen Square Incident, should not be further isolated.

Based on the above policy decision, passengers waiting at the transit room in the airport returned to the cabin after midnight on the 17th, and the aircraft carrying 208 crew and passengers left Fukuoka Airport before dawn on the 17th, and arrived in Beijing around 5 a.m. Japan time. Fourteen American passengers on the aircraft who stayed in hotels in Fukuoka City, hoping to go to the United States, also left Fukuoka Airport on the same day and headed for their destination via Narita Airport.[6]

4. Rejection of an easy solution

Although the major direction was to extradite the hijacker Zhang Zhenhai to China, there was room for more specific consideration on its method. The Law of Extradition of Japan stipulates the principle of non-extradition of political criminals, prohibition of extradition for other offenses related to political crimes, requirement of dual criminality and specific punishable injustice (Article 2). Also in terms of procedures, the law strictly stipulates the measures of the Minister for Foreign Affairs (sending a request to the Minister of Justice), the measures of the Minister of Justice (order to the Superintending Prosecutor of the Tokyo High Public Prosecutors Office), the measures of the Tokyo High Public Prosecutors Office (request to the Tokyo High Court for examination), and the examination and decision by Tokyo High Court (Article 3). Zhang Zhenhai had already declared "involvement in the Tiananmen Square Incident" as the motive for the hijacking, and if his extradition was to be examined by the Tokyo High Court, the central issue would inevitably be "whether or not he was a political prisoner". As mentioned above, it was later that the "denial of political criminality" was clearly provided for terrorist crimes, and in 1989, the possibility was not ruled out that the judiciary would make a judgment different from the government policy and say "no" to the extradition.

On the other hand, in theory, there was a method that could avoid all such complicated procedures, difficult examinations, and uncertainties in conclusions. It was a method of deporting the hijacker Zhang Zhenhai for violation of the Immigration Control Law. He was staying in a hospital in Fukuoka City because he was seriously injured at Fukuoka Airport, but he did not go through proper immigration procedures. In fact, the Fukuoka Immigration Control Bureau announced "landing prohibition measures" to Zhang Zhenhai on December 16, the day of the incident, based on the Immigration

Control Law.[7] Therefore, it would have been necessary to wait for his recovery from a humanitarian point of view, but it was possible to enter into deportation procedures under the Immigration Control Law as soon as the treatment of the injury was completed. The Immigration Control Law stipulates the procedure for deportation in its Chapter 5. Those procedures are investigation of violation, detention, examination, oral trial, and execution of deportation order, etc. The repatriation destination is "country of nationality", "country of last residence", "country of origin" or "place of birth" and in the case of Zhang Zhenhai, it was China. In other words, in theory, in the form of applying immigration control-related provisions, it was possible to draw conclusions that were substantially the same as extradition, and the procedure was to be completed within the administration and did not require the judgment of the judiciary. No conclusions could be drawn that differed from the government's policy of extraditing him to China. In a way, it was a dream way for an administrator.[8]

In fact, while the major direction of extraditing the hijacker to China was settled at an early stage, it can be seen from the media that discussions continued within the government on its method.[9] Through such discussions, it was Ichiro Komatsu, Director of the Legal Affairs Division of the Treaty Bureau of the Ministry of Foreign Affairs, who insisted that the strict procedures stipulated by the Extradition Law should be implemented rather than an easy solution. The following is a summary of the arguments that Mr. Komatsu later talked to his colleagues about, including the author.

(1) Relationship with the Hague Convention. The Convention did not stipulate the "method" of extradition of hijackers, and if it was ensured that the criminal would be handed over to the registered country of the aircraft if not prosecuted in Japan, there was no problem whether it was due to the procedures of Law of Extradition or Immigration Control Law.

(2) Due process for the protection of human rights of the hijacker. The Extradition Law of Japan provides strict procedures for

seeking the judgment of the judiciary and requirements for extradition (including provisions prohibiting extradition). These are based on the idea that even in the case of extradition; the human rights of criminals should be fulfilled. If the Government of Japan avoided complicated procedures and chose "deportation measures" based on the Immigration Control Law, which was to be completed by administrative procedures, it would greatly impair the significance of the Extradition Law that stipulated due process of the law.

(3) Domestic and foreign response. This hijacking occurred in December 1989, when the memory of the Tiananmen Square Incident was vivid, and there was extremely high internal and external concern over the treatment of criminals claimed to have been involved in the incident. If the Government of Japan took an easy solution, even if it was a dream-like approach for government officials, the decision would have led to strong criticism by academic societies, the press, Western countries including the EU, and Chinese abroad.

Based on the above arguments, the Government of Japan finally announced at a press conference by Chief Cabinet Secretary Moriyama on the morning of December 18, the third day after the incident, that the Japanese Government would proceed with the extradition procedure promptly in accordance with the Hague Convention and the Extradition Law of Japan. It was the declaration by the Government of Japan to the world that it would take a path through the narrow gate of the Extradition Law.[10]

5. Subsequent development
Since much research and reviews have already been conducted on the subsequent development of the CAAC Flight Hijacking Incident, especially the examination and decision at the Tokyo High Court, and there is no room to cover it in the scope of this paper, I would like to state only the facts in chronological order.

1989

December 19, Suspect Zhang Zhenhai transferred to the General Spinal Injuries Center in Iizuka City.

December 20, Zhang's surgery (removal of broken lumbar spine bone fragments, etc.) was completed.

December 31, Tokyo High Public Prosecutors Office transferred Suspect Zhang to Fukuoka Prison and detained him temporarily.

1990

January 11, Tokyo High Public Prosecutors Office transferred Suspect Zhang to Tokyo Detention House in Kosuge.

January 13, Zhang applied for refugee status at the Tokyo Immigration Control Bureau.

February 23, Tokyo High Public Prosecutors Office requested the Tokyo High Court to examine the extradition of Suspect Zhang.

February 27, Ministry of Justice did not approve refugee status application for Zhang and sent a disapproval notice to him.

March 23, Tokyo High Court 5th Special Division opened. The first statement of opinion.

April 2, Tokyo High Court 5th Special Division opened. The second statement of opinion.

April 4, Tokyo High Court 5th Special Division opened. The third statement of opinion. Testimony by Mr. Yue Wu, a democratic activist living in Paris. The hearing on that day ended the hearing in court.

April 20, Tokyo High Court 5th Special Department, decided that the extradition was applicable to the case.

April 25, Suspect Zhang made an immediate appeal to the Tokyo High Court for suspension of execution of the extradition order.

April 27, Tokyo High Court (Civil Part 10), dismissed the immediate appeal by Suspect Zhang.

April 28, Suspect Zhang departed from Narita Airport.

May 1, Supreme Court (First Petty Bench) dismissed Zhang's special appeal.[11]

Regarding the decision of the Tokyo High Court, the majority of academia saw it appropriate that the High Court denied political criminality by weighing the part of political motives and the serious danger to the safety of civilian aviation from the concept of "relative political crime". On the other hand, many criticize the decision that said the judicial decision would not refer to whether the extradition was appropriate or not as "too reluctant". There are also criticisms that the decision was an error in applying the Convention. There is also a commentary that pays attention to the *note verbale* issued by the Chinese government to the Japanese government during the hearing at the Tokyo High Court. In the *note verbale*, the Chinese government promised not to prosecute or punish the hijacker under Article 100 of the Chinese Criminal Code (destructive act for the purpose of anti-revolution) or Article 110 (act of vandalism of transportation) and not to investigate, prosecute or punish in relation to the Tiananmen Square Incident. That commentary takes this Chinese *note verbale* as a unilateral promise under international law.[12]

In this way, the Tokyo High Court's decisions have been evaluated by various academic societies, but these studies and discussions became possible because the Japanese government had decided to seek the judgment of the judiciary, and did not take the "easy solution" of a deportation measure immediately after the incident. Looking back at this point, I cannot help but realize the significance of the decisive role Ichiro Komatsu played in showing the practice of international law in Japan to the world.

Epilogue

In the summer of 2014, when I left China, completing the term of Envoy Extraordinary and Minister Plenipotentiary, I paid a courtesy visit to the Director-General of Department of Treaty and Law of the Ministry of Foreign Affairs of China, Mr. Xu Hong. Mr. Xu and I had been acquainted with each other for 10 years, and at the time of the final negotiations on the Japan-China Mutual Legal Assistance Treaty in August 2007, we both met as the leaders of their own negotiation teams, agreed in substance, and signed our initials at the provisional signing.

In 2014, there was one unresolved issue between the Japanese Embassy and the Ministry of Foreign Affairs of China. It was over the extradition of a Brazilian suspect in a murder case in Japan (the Brazilian suspect sent the dead body of her friend using parcel delivery service from Osaka to Tokyo and travelled to China using the passport of the victim. With a request from Japan, the suspect was detained in China. There is no Extradition Treaty between Japan and China, but there is one between Brazil and China.) In response to my departure greetings, Mr. Xu started a monologue. It was about the first encounter between him and Japan. At the time of the 1989 CAAC Flight Hijacking Incident, he visited Japan as a member of the delegation of the Ministry of Foreign Affairs of China, and faced discussions on the extradition of Zhang Zhenhai. After receiving the suspect, he said, China did not apply Article 100 (destructive act for the purpose of anti-revolution) or Article 110 (destructive act of transportation means) of the Chinese Criminal Code for prosecution or punishment, nor did they investigate, prosecute or punish in relation to the Tiananmen Square Incident. He said that, even if the relationship between the two countries is severe, cooperation based on international law could and should be promoted.

The author had the opportunity to seek direct guidance as the deputy director under the Director of the Treaty Division, Ichiro Komatsu, and as the Director of the International Convention Division and the Director of the Legal Affairs Division when Komatsu was the Deputy Director-General of the Treaty Bureau. The first thing that came to my mind when I was asked to write this memorial dissertation collection was the monologue of the Director-General of the Department of Treaty and Law of the Ministry of Foreign Affairs of China. The author left Beijing with the conviction that the seed of "putting international law into practice" sown by Mr. Ichiro Komatsu was surely growing not only in Japan but also in neighboring countries. The extradition of the Brazilian suspect to Japan was realized 2 years later in 2016.

Notes

1 For the outline of the case see *Asahi Shimbun* morning edition, December 17, 1989, p. 1.

2 Ministry of Foreign Affairs, "Conclusion of Terrorism-related Conventions" (www.mofa.go.jp).

3 *Asahi Shimbun* morning edition, December 17, 1989, p. 1.

4 Yang Zhenya, *Chushi Dongying*, Shanghai Lexicographical Publishing House / Chinese Dictionary Publishing House, January 2007.

5 *Asahi Shimbun* morning edition, December 17, 1989, p. 1.

6 *Asahi Shimbun* morning edition, December 17, 1989, p. 1, and evening edition, December 18, 1989, p. 1.

7 *Asahi Shimbun* morning edition, December 19, 1989, p. 23.

8 The Immigration Control Law also has a clause that is an enactment of the so-called "Non-refoulement Principle". The provision of Article 53-3 of the Law prohibits repatriation to a country to which the territories prescribed in Article 33-1 of the Refugee Convention of 1951 belong. Namely, territories where one's life or freedom would be threatened on account of his race, religion, nationality, membership of a particular social group or political opinion. Therefore, even in the case of deportation due to the procedure of the Immigration Control Law, the possibility of political persecution is taken into consideration, and in that sense, it is recognized that the law also shows consideration for the human rights of the parties concerned.

9 *Asahi Shimbun* morning edition, December 19, 1989, p. 3.

10 *Asahi Shimbun* evening edition, December 18, 1989, p. 15.

11 Regarding the facts, see *Asahi Shimbun* articles.

12 Yuichi Takano, "Critique of Zhang Zhenhai Extradition Case and High Court Decision", *Jurist*, No. 959 (1990), p. 62. Toyo Atsumi, "CAAC Flight Hijacking Criminals Allowed to be Extradited to the Chinese Side", *Judgment Times*, No. 726 (1990), p. 70. Yasuzou Kitamura, "Extradition of Criminals and Requests for Human Rights Standards", *The Journal of International Law and Diplomacy*, Vol. 98, No. 1, 2 (1999), p. 156. Yasuzou Kitamura, "The Concept of Relative Political Prisoners-The Zhang Zhenhai Case", in: Soji Yamamoto, Terumi Furukawa, and Yoshiro Matsui (eds), *100 Selections of International Law Judgments*, Yuhikaku, 2001, p. 106. Tadashi Imai, "The Concept of Relative Political Prisoners: The Zhang Zhenhai Case", Akira Kotera, Koichi Morikawa, and Yumi Nishimura (eds), *100 Selections of International Law Judgments*, 2nd ed, Yuhikaku, 2011, p. 98. Kazuhiro Nakatani, *Law School / International Law Reader*, Shinzansha, 2013, p. 8.

Epilogue

In September 2001, I was asked by the Waseda University Graduate School of Law to give a lecture to graduate students as a part-time lecturer. As the Director of the Legal Affairs Division of the Ministry of Foreign Affairs, I was working on everyday diplomatic issues from the perspective of international law, so giving a weekly lecture to graduate students of the leading private university in Japan was an extremely challenging invitation. At that time, I was in charge of "connecting the Ministry of Foreign Affairs and the International Law Society", so there were many opportunities to exchange opinions with professors, like chairing the International Law Study Group at the Ministry of Foreign Affairs four times a year, and monthly international law study sessions with a limited number of professors. There were many heated arguments about diplomatic issues at such meetings. Still, those were discussions of international law practitioners facing daily diplomatic issues and differed from the scholar's point of view conducting the theory and judicial precedent studies.

From the fall of that year to the next spring, and from the fall of the following year to the spring of 2003, I visited Waseda University every Saturday and organized a seminar with more than a dozen graduate students. At the seminar, I assigned each student a diplomatic issue that Japan was facing and asked them to present the case, the government's judgment, its background, and their evaluation under international law while I was giving comments on the presentation. However, those discussions with graduate students turned out to be unexpectedly shocking to me. There is no problem if the evaluation of cases under international law and the student's arguments are different from those of the government. Because that is the discussion that should be held in a free academic institution, and it is the only way to enhance each other. However, as a problem before such arguments, the students had no understanding at all of how the government perceived the issues under international law and what kind of logic it had created to handle the case.

Naturally, my initial reaction was, "Don't young people these days study anything?" However, as the discussions continued, I was struck by the question of how graduate students could get to know the government's thinking. The government's official views were clarified through various forms, such as the Chief Cabinet Secretary's daily press conference, the Foreign Minister's press conference, the Prime Minister and ministers' response at the Diet sessions and the written response from the government, but it is not the case that all of them are reported to the media. In the Ministry of Foreign Affairs, we often organize our logic in the form of a Question & Answer, and when submitting a treaty to the Diet for its approval, we collect Questions & Answers and create a book that can be called a commentary. However, if no specific question is actually asked, there will be no specific answer to it expressed. This results in the fact that it is impossible to measure how the government organized the logic on those issues from the outside. In other words, the fact that students did not know the government's way of analyzation and evaluating under international law was not due to their lack of study but to the lack of explanation or unconscious negligence of government officials, including me. Those were my findings.

From such reflection, I wrote a dissertation on one maritime incident and had it read by Professor Yukio Shimada of Waseda University. He praised the article, advising me strongly to print it and arranged to publish it in "Waseda Law Review". Similarly, Professor Kazuhiro Nakatani of Tokyo University and Professor Masahiko Asada of Kyoto University gave me warm reviews and allowed me to print some of my dissertations. In that way, I have written several papers intending to get Japanese people to understand the practice of international law as accurately as possible. When I was appointed as the Ambassador Extraordinary and Plenipotentiary to the Kingdom of the Netherlands, a plan came to my mind to translate some of those papers into English and provide them to academics around the world. Fortunately, H.E. Judge Yuji Iwasawa of the International Court of Justice gave me the foreword, and Leiden University Press, the publishing department of my wife's alma mater, agreed to publish the book. I cannot thank enough all the people who have supported me so far.

In addition, I would like to mention that I have lost very important friends during my practice of international law through these years. Mr. Makoto Matsuda, who supported me as an assistant director in the postwar proceedings, Mr. Shinichi Iida, who survived the harsh media scrum with me as the principal deputy director in the Shenyang Consulate-General case, Professor Yasuaki Onuma of Tokyo University, who had invited me to his study group for a presentation, and Mr. Ichiro Komatsu, who kindly taught me as the director of the Treaties Division and the deputy director-general of the Treaties Bureau, have all passed away. I have also lost Ambassador Xu Hong of China, who became a colleague and a friend in Beijing and the Netherlands. "Flowers bloom the same way every year, but people do not remain the same" (Tang poetry by Liu Xiyi). While swearing to my heart to further build up the practice of international law that I have built with these friends, I would like to put my pen aside here.

Printed and bound by CPI Group (UK) Ltd, Croydon, CR0 4YY

09/06/2025

14685748-0002